About the author

DJ, producer, tour manager and now chancing it
as an author.

DJS ON TOUR — SURVIVING THE FAST LANE

Ross Evans

DJS ON TOUR — SURVIVING THE FAST LANE

Vanguard Press

A CIP catalogue record for this title is
available from the British Library.

ISBN 978-1-80016-119-1

Vanguard Press is an imprint of
Pegasus Elliot MacKenzie Publishers Ltd.
www.pegasuspublishers.com

First Published in 2021

Vanguard Press
Sheraton House Castle Park
Cambridge England

Printed & Bound in Great Britain

Dedication

This book is dedicated to my friend, Paul Strange, aka "The Mad Mohawk", who gave me my first break in music, and who sadly passed away on 9 December 2019.

Prologue

"Why does it always happen to you?" Dubfire had asked after the suicide attempt in Thailand. Not my suicide, just my problem.

I started to wonder, lying in that bleak metal bed, trying to block the smell of bleach, bodily excretions, and hospital gravy from entering my battered lungs, why *did* it happen to me? I've never stopped to think about it before.

I'd simply never stopped until pneumonia stopped me in 2019. It does that when left untreated; it fills your lungs with poison and empties your batteries. I tried to honour my gigs but relinquished my DJ equipment a month later and headed to the hospital, sick of blacking out, weak and wounded, heart palpitating. My heart had been beating so fast for weeks I didn't even know I'd had a heart attack until the doctor told me.

There was no chance of missing the next one, wired up to an ECG monitor with pacemakers all over me, the only beats I'd be generating for a while. The old fella next door kept shitting himself, and people were screaming; it took me back to the girl who did a shit on the dance floor of Home Sydney, and I allowed myself a small chuckle. Laughing hurt, but I'd just written my will, so I didn't have a great deal to giggle about. I'm no quitter, but I'd accepted the fact that I might never get better; at least I had no kids to leave fatherless.

So why did it always happen to me? I'd certainly lived. I'd toured the globe with the best DJs, released over one hundred and twenty tracks, heard my music blasted across Brazilian beaches, and even done Around The World in ten days with Nic Fanciulli. It was like a dream come true, a twenty-four-seven roller coaster of a dream that was now becoming a nightmare as events unfolded that would put my survival skills to the test. I couldn't even get to sleep, let alone wake up from it.

I didn't want to go out like this, shoved in a corner in an overcrowded hospital of death. I'd rather have died of altitude sickness or a broken bungee string. Or at least died comfortably in my king-size bed. All I wanted was to escape Ward 17, rest at home with the right medication, and will my energy back. So I begged my way out of there, with plenty of time to muse over Dubfire's question as my body tried to repair the damage of the last fifteen years.

Tour manager. DJ. Producer. Non-stop. While reflecting on the madness that became my life, I started to write. My strength was slowly gathering, so I went to spa hotels to give my lungs some love. Reclining on various daybeds, over the next two months, nosy neighbours gaped openly at the words on my laptop, staring in unconcealed wonderment at the pacemakers I still wore while charting my musical pilgrimage through life, still suffering quietly. Looking like a suicide bomber in a dressing gown, all flights were grounded.

Soon I had even more time to reflect, from a less luxurious bed made purely of plastic, surrounded by an entirely different cast of inmates. Anything had to be better than the panic attacks and delirium that were accompanying my alleged recovery, but how did I wind up with a load of alcoholics and heroin addicts?

"What you in here for?" they'd ask. Like jail, which I'd narrowly avoided a few years back when life took a dive into dark waters. Sleep was all I ever wanted, a good old-fashioned sleep, without worrying whether the police would be waiting for me on the runway when another journey ended. I'd done so many journeys; around the world, from private jets to McDonald's drive-thrus.

Many people assume the DJ life is pure sex, drugs and rock 'n' roll. Occasionally they're right, but it's mostly a lonely nomadic existence, segregated from the action in the DJ booth or locked in dark basements making tracks. But after thousands of gigs, meeting the weird, the wired, and wonderful people of Planet Earth, eventually, interesting things happen. In some cases — wild things.

But for now, the wild times were over, confined to my flat in the face of covid in locked-down London. The year 2020 had such a nice ring to it. I got that creative feeling back, had ideas to start releasing music, and put some tours together when every music venue in the world closed down, and DJs went back to their bedrooms. The last time the music industry was affected like that was during the eruption of the Icelandic volcano in 2010 and the global recession of 2008. I am being grounded these days more than I was when I was a child.

My three favourite things: music, restaurants, and travel had been taken away — again, along with my free spirit and global-minded way of thinking. In return, I received the gift of time. My life was travelling at one hundred miles per hour, never stopping. Only when I got sick did I stop, reflect, and have time to relax, to think, to cook the meals I learnt in Bangkok, and write this book. Now I was into my own second lockdown, this time with everyone else in with me.

Had I continued living the rock star lifestyle, I would never have moved on as a person. It took being hospitalised, rehab, and lockdown to do it. Pneumonia knocked something out of me, maybe lost forever, but I wasn't going to let it take away my memories: the madness, the glorious gladness, sadness, and brilliant badness of life on the road.

How did it all start? It started with an inherently different kind of journey. Not the one down my mother's birth canal to Newport, Wales, in 1976. Not the journey from Wales to Bristol in my mate's antique Ford Escort on my eighteenth birthday. It was the flawless melodic odyssey that Sasha conducted that same night at Lakota.

The tracks he pulled out of his record bag were unlike anything I'd heard: progressive, layered, and epic as it comes, with huge melodic breakdowns. I'd listened to rave cassettes before, but it all finally made sense when I found myself on the dance floor in Lakota.

I'd never experienced anything like that vibe or those tunes, the offers of drinks, cigarettes, and Tiger Balm massages, sweaty smiles and numbers scribbled on flyers. I only had enough cash for one bottle of water the whole night, but it didn't matter. I'd only ever known Newport's streets full of fighting drunks and school discos, and Ritzy's under-eighteen nights playing non-stop shit pop. Looking back, the pills must have been strong because the sound system was rattling, and the toilets made your nose sting. But it was 1995. It was raw, it was underground, and it was meant to be dark and dingy. We had the time of our lives at that rave.

I became a regular at Lakota. No-one blew me away quite like Sasha, but Laurent Garnier came close with his never-heard-before trippy techno and French flair and John Digweed's deep progressive emotional marathons. I was mesmerised by Sasha that night, lulled along by his electronic lullaby. Staring up at the DJ booth while my mates stomped on the dance floor, my ears were milking every last drop of precision executed perfection, wondering where on earth he got his music from and trying to figure out just how he was doing it and if I could do it myself.

The soundtrack to our night was an electronic sci-fi soundscape of pure brilliance that held me captivated from the beginning until the end.

This was what I wanted to be doing.

We Love Space Ibiza

May 2004, I was strolling back to my new Ibiza apartment in Figueretas, the sky turning a peachy shade of pink. There were two girls behind me, shouting in Spanish. At first it seemed the perfect place to live, in between Ibiza Town and Playa d'en Bossa with golden sands and not quite crystal-clear waters, kebab shops on every corner, and no shortage of *locuterias* to top up your phone or use the internet. But there was no shortage of sex and drugs on the streets, night or day, when wolf-whistling African girls stood on corners in tiny skirts, trying to grab me as I walked home. I assumed these two were prostitutes, so I picked up my pace, but when they switched to English, I turned around and realised that they were not the usual street girls; they were typically skinny Eastern European chicks wearing shorts and flip-flops like any other beautiful Ibiza party person.

It was May, early days in Ibiza. I was new and knew nobody, so when they asked if I wanted a drink, I thought, *Why not?* We sat talking for an hour; they were big fans of electronic music and had spent time in the Greek Islands, Barcelona and Paris, like me. They loved London as much as I loved Bucharest, and when they asked if I could get the Space tags that secured free entry all summer, I gave them my number.

"Sorry for ignoring you earlier. I thought you were prostitutes," I admitted with a smile, feeling guilty for judging them.

"We are prostitutes." They grinned. "This is our night off. Welcome to Ibiza."

"Thanks," I said, trying to keep my smile intact as I signalled to the waiter. I paid the bill, waved goodbye, and spent the rest of the summer trying to avoid them.

I was working for We Love Sundays at Space, dubbed by the music press as the hottest party on the island. It was hard graft, flyering the streets in soaring temperatures, watching over my shoulder, or taking respite in the back of a police car while my flyers were confiscated, but driving the DJs on Sundays made it all worthwhile.

A few weeks previously, I'd almost given up on my Ibiza dream. Fresh from my travels in Australia, I'd booked a one-week package holiday to find an apartment before the masses arrived. With barely any money and a £24,000 university debt, *El Diario* newspaper was the main place to find accommodation, but my Spanish was so bad I struggled to translate the adverts, let alone negotiate the rent.

I'd been exploring Asia and Australasia since graduating with a marketing degree, DJing at Home nightclub, and PRing on Bondi Beach. I was followed by the *Australia Uncovered* crew for a few days, which was screened to the world, flyering the beach in between marketing jobs for MSN Hotmail. My adventures had opened my mind to bigger things; I didn't want the standard nine-to-five office job with the same dudes at their desks every day. I didn't want to fall straight into a monotonous UK life. Australia had thrown so many opportunities at me, working for Home with The Mad Mohawk and Pommy Johnny; DJing at Tank, Gas, Goldfish, and The Greenwood. In Melbourne, I played at Brown Alley and Revolver, Capulet in Brisbane, Platinum on the Gold Coast, and Noodle Palace in Perth. But still, it wasn't enough. I desperately wanted to make it work in music on a global scale. Travel included. My old mate Pistol Pete put me in touch with Darren Hughes, the promoter of We Love, who offered me a job.

On the sixth day of my seven-day deadline, I hadn't found anywhere to live, and it was looking like I would be flying back home. Then, I spotted a handwritten note on a coffee shop window for a small shabby studio flat *con* mosquito nest. There was a brothel next door, unbeknown to me until I saw my new Eastern European friends in tight dresses and towering heels when I left to collect Sasha for the first time. It was a nerve-racking wait at the airport, wondering if it was cool to play the Sasha mix tape I'd been rinsing out or extremely uncool. But I soon realised DJs didn't want to hear music in the car with me. Once I got Sasha on the subjects of football and music, two Welshmen with the same dark sense of humour laughed all the way to Space.

Suddenly my heroes were sitting in my car on a weekly basis: Danny Tenaglia, Laurent Garnier, Fatboy Slim, Sasha, and John Digweed, telling me where they'd flown in from and relaying crazy tales, asking me what was happening on the island — which parties were booming and the top tracks of the summer. David Guetta actually noted my answers on his phone: Underground on Wednesdays, Monza, DC10 and Cocoon. M.A.N.D.Y and Booka Shade's "Body Language" and Loco Dice's "Seeing through Shadows" (although I couldn't imagine them working at Fuck Me I'm Famous). The only time I didn't have Tiefschwarz or Sasha blasting out the speakers was when the big boys were in the car, resting their ears before the gig.

Very rarely did the DJs venture out of their hotel until I picked them up. Their main contact outside the club was me. DJs I'd travelled far and wide to see, all over the UK since 1995, France, Spain and Portugal from 1999 and Australia and New Zealand from 2000. Space, on a Sunday, was smashing it for twenty-two hours every week, and I was driving the DJs for the entire party, often the only person who could maintain a normal conversation. Most partygoers are so drug-fucked or star-struck that many of the big DJs just switch off and focus on playing. I was only a low-level driver and PR guy, but they started inviting me places:

dinner parties with Kate Moss and the Pet Shop Boys, afterparties with Leonardo DiCaprio and Diddy.

Diddy showed up to rap over Felix da Housecat's set one Sunday, and his ten-strong crew of morons pushed us We Love staff out of the DJ booth, then complained about the lack of hospitality. But the rest of the artists and celebs were super polite. I turned up on time, didn't get wasted, drove them home when they needed a ride, told them the secret sunset spots, and they treated me as an equal — like I was important. The money still sucked, but I knew something better was coming.

I'd been driving Steve Lawler around when four weeks into summer he asked me to be his tour manager. I had little idea what this job entailed, but after one phone call, my gut told me to put the DJing aside. Working at We Love left Fridays and Saturdays free, making me the perfect candidate for touring Friday and Saturday and flying back for his Space residency on Sundays. I remembered Richard Branson's words about taking a chance. I'd read *Losing my Virginity* during the twenty-three-hour flight back from Oz, finishing as we landed at Heathrow. It was the most inspirational book I've read: how to make a living out of the fun stuff, nothing mundane, that could eventually become a livelihood. That was his narrative: record labels, pop stars, airlines — it just had to be fun. His most famous quote: "Nothing ventured, nothing gained," remains in my mind to this day.

If Everyone Hates You, You're Doing Your Job

I knew how to play the tunes and rock the party, but did I know how to be a tour manager? I wasn't so sure about that, so I phoned my mate, Patrick — Sasha's and John Digweed's tour manager.

"Ross, you'll pick it up as you go along," he said. "But let me tell you one thing: If everyone hates you, you're doing your job."

The first weekend we took a private jet to Portugal. I'd been sent the itinerary by the agent and been fully briefed over a glass of wine at Steve's villa. A DJ set up is standard for most DJs; most of the guys I've worked with use Traktor — amazing DJ software, but it can be like a time bomb, flick the wrong switch, and it's all over. There are tricky soundcards and other bits of hardware, but I already knew the technical stuff and did my homework on the gigs. I'd spoken to the promoters, and everything was set.

As I walked across the tarmac that day, it was hot and humid, with that undefinable Ibiza Airport smell hovering in the air. It felt surreal. A plane that was actually waiting for us? No rush to the airport? The late Erick Morillo had lent us his slick four-man jet for the weekend, and the captain saluted us as we drew near. I returned the gesture, travelling in luxury for the first time in my life. There is nothing like a salute to make you feel respected.

In the middle of four phat leather seats was a bucket with two bottles of Dom Pérignon. We cracked them open once airborne and finished both bottles in no time. Eventually came the question, "Where's the toilet?" The captain turned around with apologetic eyebrows.

My first official tour manager duty was emptying a champagne bucket to create a makeshift toilet. I had to hide at the back of the jet and close my eyes and ears while the bucket was filled up again. An hour later, it was my turn; soon, we had a bucket full of piss accompanying us to Madeira. Luckily, it was a smooth landing, and nothing was spilt on that plush, creamy carpet.

When the captain cut the engines, we could hear the music vibrating under the runway. A car took us from the jet, down below ground, to a massive subterranean space underneath the runway, like nothing I've seen before, or since, open to the elements on each side. There was a huge rig, and sky-scraping columns seemed to hold the runway up, with scaffolding podiums for the dancers and projections.

Five thousand people were waiting, and once Steve started playing, every single face was fixed on him playing cutting-edge tech house with cool melodies, with lasers slicing and spinning through the atmosphere.

I later learnt that the Portuguese go out late, so landing at four a.m. was the perfect time, and they don't leave until the music stops, which on this occasion was eight a.m. Like a warehouse that wasn't a warehouse, the underground vibes and industrial outdoor setting were totally unique. During the last thirty minutes of the set, daylight leaked across the crowd and revealed a rugged volcanic landscape as the sun rose over the sea.

During the party, the jet was waiting for us on the runway above, and after he finished, we were driven back up to it. We flew to Barcelona for the next gig, and I was quickly into life on tour. We didn't touch the champagne this time. Or the bucket.

The gigs kept on coming — it was relentless. In the first month of the job, I'd travelled to eight countries, staying in super-swanky hotels. The Hotel Arts in Barcelona was ranked in the top five hotels in the world at the time. It was an unbelievable place where you clapped one way for the lights and a different way for the blinds. The Park Hyatt in Milan was absolute luxury, Hotel de Rome in Berlin mixed German efficiency with Italian elegance, and the Sofitel in Munich had beds like marshmallows. I even got to stay in the Park Hyatt in Tokyo, where they filmed *Lost in Translation*, one of my favourite movies; I imagined the scene when Bill Murray gets kinky with a prostitute from an identical-looking room.

We travelled to Italy almost incessantly that summer. The electronic music scene was at its peak, and their outdoor clubs were on another level. The job wasn't rocket science; it was an endurance test. I always had to be on the ball and three steps ahead of my DJ and the promoter. A full night's sleep was not an option on the road — we were lucky to get three hours, and we were off again. I can't sleep on planes, which was a huge disadvantage. My DJ was often fast asleep before take-off, and I was wide awake until landing.

Sometimes we arrived at the airport, and there was no driver to pick us up and nobody answering the phone. Technical riders, which list the equipment the promoter needs to provide and organise sound checks and itineraries, seemed of no importance to some of the trickier promoters, but as many of them were Mafia-connected, I had to be careful. They needed us to fill their club; we needed them to look after us. Even when we had no idea what time we were playing or when we'd be picked up, somehow, it always came together at the last minute. It was disorganised chaos, but everyone was making money, and the gigs were banging, so no-one complained.

In the beginning, I was naïve, but I soon learnt the tricks. Promoters often told me that our requested hotel was full; I'd check online and see that it wasn't, just expensive. "Do you think I'm stupid? Start being honest." It was clear that not everyone was trustworthy like me; I had to be ready for all kinds of shady behaviour.

One day, a promoter in Lecce, South Italy, gave us a cash flow sob story and begged to pay us on the night, in cash, at the hotel before the gig. A rule of thumb in the DJ world is that if the DJ fee hasn't been paid, you don't board the plane, but we knew this guy, so we agreed on this occasion. I was waiting in the hotel lobby for his driver to bring the money, ringing the promoter, until three hours later, he promised to give me the money from the door.

We had to make a decision. If you don't show up, the fans feel let down. In 2004 there was no Facebook or Instagram, so we couldn't post on social media that the promoter hadn't paid us to force his hand. We decided to go ahead, and I agreed to collect the cash at the club. The driver showed up at the last minute and took us to a heaving outdoor venue like a Roman amphitheatre; hundreds of people were swaying in sync on the dance floor and reaching for the skies around the sides. The lighting was minimal, no dancers or effects — just a crowd who went wild for the music; they worshipped Steve in Italy. When the sun came up, the place came alive as people got chatting and joking — just like the Space Terrace. His residency at Space was pioneering a new global sound that had the groove; it had emotion.

At seven a.m. when the music stopped, there was no sign of the promoter — or the money. The club finished, and everyone went home. The driver who was waiting couldn't speak a word of English, but somehow understood when I told him very firmly to take me to the promoter. Now. The local tour promoter was randomly an old friend from my hometown; I hadn't seen him for ten years but spotted his name on the itinerary the day before the gig. As we say in our town, "You can take the boy out of Newport, but you can't take Newport out of the boy."

The driver showed us to an office where I could hear guys' voices inside; I knocked on the door repeatedly, but no answer. I knocked a few more times, just to be polite, then we smashed it open. It was like a scene from Pablo Escobar's mansion with the two promoters hiding behind large mounds of cocaine and cash. Had Italy not just changed from lira to euros, the office would not have been big enough to fit all that money. We shouted until they gave us what we were owed, got back in the car, and went to the hotel for a few hours' sleep. Next day, the driver didn't show up to take us to the airport, presumably the promoter's goodwill goodbye message.

Patrick's words were echoing in my ears on the plane home. DJing was about giving out good vibes and incredible sounds to entertain the dance floor, but when you reach a certain level, you need someone to do your dirty work: kicking people off the stage or out of the DJ booth, negotiating with airlines that had cancelled our flights, and finding new rooms when receptionists looked blankly at us. When I was the DJ, I could be myself, dishing out the drinks, playing the music everybody loved, and only giving out good vibes, but as soon as I stepped into the role of tour manager, I needed a hard exterior. I was always fair, but in a huge crowd, when the majority were high on pills and acting like jerks, someone had to bring some kind of order, or things get out of hand. Most people didn't like it when I told them what they didn't want to hear. "You can't steal the DJ's drinks. Or his spare headphones. You need to leave the DJ booth. Now, please." Served with a smile that never reached my eyes. They'd beg and plead, then often switch completely to play the hard man, squaring up to me with their googly eyes. I don't know if people acted so irrationally because they were wasted or simply because they were full-time retards. I soon got used to it.

I spent more time with my DJs than they do with their wives or girlfriends, so ultimately there were ups and downs at airports, delayed flights causing chaos, suffering from sleep deprivation. As a tour manager, you fix whatever comes your way, ensure everything possible is done to make the gig, and try to do it with zero mistakes. I was learning fast that you do your gig, fly to the next one, reset your mind, and start again. It doesn't matter if the gig was good or bad, if you had fun or not, whether you had problems or if everything went smoothly; you wake up in the morning (or continue through the night, as was often the case) and start a new day. It's the only way to do it. Don't hold grudges —

the scene is too small — but you learn who to keep in your life and who to lose.

Somehow, I was still doing the flyering job Mondays to Thursdays, tour managing Fridays and Saturdays, and driving the DJs to Space on Sundays. I honoured the Space job, but I was counting down to the weekends. To get back on the road, to places I'd seen on TV but never dreamed I'd go to: Austria, Russia, Portugal, Montenegro, Malta, Serbia, Slovenia, and Switzerland; to places I'd never heard of such as Mamaia in Romania, Crimea, Pula in Croatia, Sunny Beach in Bulgaria, and every town in Italy.

I was fascinated by new cultures, new people, and new cuisines. The promoters knew the best local places to eat, so I started requesting these more rustic restaurants and making a note of where I went, all around the world. When friends went travelling, I was the first one they'd ask for tips. Back then, Tripadvisor didn't exist, so I was a helpful asset, with lists of all the best restaurants for most major cities in my phone. London, New York, Paris, Chicago, Miami, Barcelona, Berlin, Moscow, Los Angeles, Tokyo, Bali, Rome, Sydney, Melbourne, Ibiza, Mykonos, Bangkok, Amsterdam, and Madrid are places I know almost as well as my hometown. There are hundreds of restaurants on my lists — from Tickets in Barcelona and Insight in Moscow to Penny Lane in Bali, Amazonico in London, and Scorpios in Mykonos.

I was starting to feel like a global citizen. I didn't live or belong anywhere any more, but I felt at home wherever I was. I was just as comfortable hanging out with a bunch of Swedes as a gang of Argentinians. It didn't matter where people came from; the more different they were, the more interesting for me. We always had at least one thing in common: music.

Ibiza Hedonism

Summer was flying by, each week getting hotter and steamier. Sundays at Space were rocking — everyone on the island would come down, and some would fly far and wide to be there. One DJ had been flying in from Chicago every few weeks and had become a crowd favourite that summer. Not only for his music but for his charisma, aura, and sheer hedonism. He was an absolute riot — notorious for his flamboyancy — he lived his life as if every day was his last. I think I took some of that from him. He and I had a great connection, and he always requested me to look after him. Trouble.

"Ross, please take me directly to Veronica's," he said upon arriving one time.

"What's 'Veronica's'?"

He directed me to a small apartment near Pacha and told me to come in with him. An old lady answered the door who smiled as if she recognised him and politely showed us in. I could hear girls giggling and gossiping in another room. The old lady left and came back with about twenty South American girls in bikinis and introduced them one by one.

"Ross, pick four girls to come to the club with us," he said, to my dismay. It was a viewing deck, and it was my first time in a brothel. I was a bit uncomfortable, but the DJ was pretty adamant, so I chose the most exotic ones: natural beauties with long dark hair, tall and leggy, giving me their most alluring smiles, perfect pouts, and fluttering lashes.

I waited in the car while the DJ settled the bill. He came back and told me to pick him up at two a.m. from his hotel and then collect the girls. "Just don't tell anyone they're hookers," he said.

I picked him up at two on the dot and drove to Veronica's, where the girls were waiting. The chosen four were apparently the only four from Brazil; they piled into my car, and we set off to Space, smelling like a cheap perfume shop. The DJ started playing to a full dance floor, with his four-girl entourage prancing around him. They looked like ducks out of water. None of them spoke a word of English, and they clearly didn't listen to electronic music, let alone dance to it. They were moving strangely out of time, in the shortest dresses. Had they ever stepped foot in a club before?

"Who are these girls? They're hookers, right?" became the recurring question of the night. It was so blatantly obvious that after a few hours, I gave up lying, ignored all questions and simply smiled. After his set finished, the troupe bundled back into the car, and I drove them to the Pacha Hotel.

The DJ said, "Thanks for tonight, Ross. You're a good guy. To show my appreciation, you're taking those two, and I'm taking these." He informed the girls of his wicked plan and walked two of them to the lift, leaving me standing awkwardly with *mine*. Suddenly he had a quick change of heart, switched two around with a grin, and disappeared behind closing doors.

So I followed orders and took them back to my shabby but not-so-chic studio flat. I hadn't seen money change hands, so it didn't feel like prostitution to me, and why not give it a whirl? There's a first time for everything. I stocked up on vodka and mixers at the local supermarket, and we drained the lot during our wild boozy morning, but sadly their dancing skills didn't improve. I can't say I cared; with two smooth-skinned Brazilians on my hands, the total language barrier forced us to find new ways to communicate. I'm happy to say I rose to the challenge.

I woke up around eleven a.m., and the girls had vanished, perhaps comparing notes with the two that bagged the more glamorous end of the deal. Somewhat surprisingly, my wallet and valuables were intact, and I felt OK. My neighbours must have seen the girls leave as they flashed me a knowing wink. Next time I tried to swerve them, knowing, it seemed, that I was falling into a high-flying world of hedonism and hookers, drugs and booze.

I picked up one French DJ from the airport who asked me to drop him at Ibiza Town for five minutes before taking him to his hotel. I jokingly asked if he was going to buy crack and he kind of half laughed at me. When I went back to his hotel later that night, he didn't come down. I could smell it when I got out of the lift, that chemical stench of burning plastic. His door was wide open, and he was lying on his floor, completely cracked-out, holding some kind of séance with two friends. I tapped the door gently.

"Are you thinking of getting ready to play your set?" I enquired, with what would become my tour manager smile. His empty features told me he'd forgotten why he was in Ibiza, and what his name was, but when I reminded him, he somehow got dressed and played an extremely trippy five a.m. set in the dark room of Space. It was pretty impressive, and nobody knew any different. How he pulled it off, I don't know. He could hardly see.

Like many of the people who visited Ibiza that summer and came to We Love Sundays at Space — models, drug gangs, footballers, ladyboys, and movie stars — I was often invited to their phone-free afterparties; a single snapshot at the wrong moment could have ruined their careers. I guess they trusted me because I spoke to them like normal people and never tried to take advantage or sell their drug-taking stories. I've since been to Colombia and Peru many times, but I've never seen drug consumption as rife as in Ibiza. It's totally out of control. Every second person I met was a dealer, and most of the bars were selling narcotics.

The year 2004 was when ketamine hit Ibiza's clubs, coffee tables, toilet cubicles, and DJs. When the new minimal sound was being pioneered by Cocoon and

DC10, K was blatantly being keyed out of bags while avoiding the giant fans that cooled the dance floors. Monday was my day off, so I went to both these parties every week. Daytime at DC10 started like the social club of the island, fooling around on the terrace in streaming sunshine. Later it got so stupidly packed that putting your hands in the air risked not getting them down again. Once the socialising was out of the way, Ibiza's workers and key players got seriously lost in the music, often after We Love's long-distance Sunday session. One of the first questions I always had to answer was, "What time are you going to Cocoon?" While refusing a line of K.

Many of the big DJs were taking so much K that their performance was like a lottery. Sometimes they were so into the music they were at one with it; other times, they were so K holed-up they couldn't read the crowd. They couldn't read the label on a bottle of beer.

Cocoon at Amnesia was immense; the sound was so special, and the music, next level, in a huge hangar-style venue packed to the rafters right up to the terraces. The main room was booming with a big graphic equaliser strapped across the DJ booth, pulsing with the beat as the bass throbbed through the dance floor. I loved to stand at the top, looking down on a mass of bobbing heads, intermittently lit up by strobes and crazy visuals. The terrace, even though no longer open-air, still had that terrace feeling, not too heavy with a crisp, fresh sound. When the early morning sun came in through the glass roof, you saw people's smiles instead of dancing with strangers in the dark.

I regularly ended up with strangers because my group of friends loved their ketamine. The more minimal the music, the more they connected with it, and the further they drifted from me. I was the only one just drinking, so I got used to people being distant. One of the urban myths circulating clubland since it arrived on the scene is that ketamine is a tranquilliser used to sedate horses. I can't imagine how horses handle it, but the people who do it become completely disconnected from those around them and hardly ever communicate. Sometimes I was the only person in the entire club not on K; everybody around me was totally incoherent. We would start the night at someone's house, joking around, but as soon as the K took hold, the conversation ended. Not exactly my idea of fun; when I'm at a party, I want to socialise with my eyes open and have a laugh. But this was my crowd; they were good people, they loved music, and I was in Ibiza, not Singapore, so I had to get used to it. Some of the crew included Jamie Jones and Richy Ahmed — great guys who went on to become huge DJ's. I am very happy to see their success, especially Jamie who is a fellow Welshman. It's always nice to see a Welshman do good.

I rarely take drugs but tried most when I was purely a party goer: speed, ecstasy, marijuana, cocaine, 2CV, mushrooms and LSD. The fact that I've tried them means that I understand the behaviour of people who are on them, how they're thinking and why they act as they do. I can tell instantly what someone is on and speak to them appropriately. Even if I choose not to do it myself, I can understand why people do, the same way I understand why people drink to escape the monotony or smoke weed to relax. As a DJ, it's essential to know how people are feeling to get on that wavelength with your music. I never took anything when I was working as a tour manager as I had to keep my head on, especially if my DJ was wasted.

I'm more of a drinker myself, a drinker who learnt to train his mind. Driving the DJs non-stop for twenty-two hours became gruelling, despite the cool conversations with electronic music legends. I'd drink the odd beer during breaks, and if I started to feel tipsy, I had to snap right out of it when called into action. When I DJ, I drink to feel invincible on the decks, but you're concentrating so hard that you never get drunk until you finish your set. As a tour manager, I had to be alert at all times, so I never switched off. If you never relax your mind, you don't get drunk. Relaxing was not part of the job.

At the end of summer, the owner rewarded me for my hard work with an afternoon set on the Space Terrace. I couldn't sleep the night before. It wasn't just the Space Terrace; it was the We Love Sundays at Space Terrace — the most famous dance floor in the world. I must have been the only person to play there who had not touched the decks for three months, and I couldn't even drink to calm my nerves because I had to drive the DJs until six a.m. The crew came early to see me play, and I was surprised to see so many party people on the dance floor, but the first week of September always attracted those on their second holiday with cash to burn.

My hands shook as I tried to drop the needle on the first record. And missed it again. But within ten minutes, I was into my groove. The sun was blazing through the glass roof, and Ibiza's beautiful people were all smiles, big sunglasses, and hands in the air. It was the best feeling of my life so far: to provide the soundtrack that kept them moving on that iconic terrace. I kept it groovy and melodic to suit the sunny surroundings and please as many people as possible, stragglers from the night before and fresh faces coming in. I'd learnt how to play the room from watching the other DJs.

It was the year that I'd started to learn about cutting-edge music, hanging with the DJs who played it, on and off duty. I got into more organic-sounding music with cool melodies and layers — the German sound was taking over, artists like Tiefschwarz were our residents, and their musical influence was rubbing off on me. If you'd told me five years ago that I'd be playing the hallowed Space Terrace, I'd have laughed. I was buzzing for weeks with the confidence that if I could play there, I could play anywhere.

Escaping Reality

From dropping a few flyers on the sand, life had evolved into that of a superstar DJ (although I wasn't quite there yet), picking hookers from a line-up and knowing anyone who's anyone on the scene. I was well aware that summer would finish, and it would all stop when Steve's brother reclaimed his job unless I made something happen. Space closed, and I was jobless.

So I went back to Australia for one final summer, back to promoting Home nightclub with The Mad Mohawk during the last of the post-Olympics glory years in Sydney. When I walked back into the club, it was magic. The sound system was on point, and the regulars were like family, warmly welcoming me back with that Aussie hospitality, and they couldn't wait to hear my Ibiza stories.

One night at Home forever stays in my mind for all the wrong reasons. It was a huge Saturday night; we were up on the terrace where we used to hang, overlooking a rocking main room. To the left of the DJ booth, a girl was staggering about, eyes rolling, until she steadied herself against the wall. I kept an eye on her, but she was still upright and was with a group of friends.

Suddenly, she rolled up her pink Lycra dress, crouched down and hovered a few inches above the dance floor. Surely, she couldn't be taking a shit? She then stood up with a little wobble, pulled her dress down, put her hands in the air and started dancing. *No-one would do a dump on the dance floor at Home Sydney*, I thought, when the most evil stench, wafted my way. Suddenly she seemed to realise what she'd done and tried to clean it up with her bare hands. But what to do with it? Looking around with increasing agitation, she started wiping it across the walls; it was all over her hands when she fell into the wall and coated herself. I couldn't believe what I was seeing. The people around her started freaking out, screaming and gagging, backing away from the stink with their hands to their mouths.

Our resident DJ (Pommy) Jonny kept playing while she smeared shit over the wall next to his DJ booth, utterly horrified. I could see Paul's massive green mohawk bobbing in the main room; I never ever saw him dance — just bob. He noticed the mass exit and started to walk against the flow when his look of concern switched to utter disgust, face crumpling as he broke into a run and got on the walkie-talkie to security.

We never saw her after that. It was an interesting night for the cleaners who had more than the usual collection of crap to clean up, but it was too late — the vibe was killed, the dance floor had cleared. News spread like wildfire; within minutes, I was getting messages from friends in London asking if it was true that a girl had actually shit on the dance floor of Home Sydney.

I pitied the poor taxi driver taking her home, the state of his taxi, and how she'd feel when she woke up. I truly hoped she was a backpacker who could move on the next day rather than a local who might never live it down for the rest of her life.

It was great to see the Aussie gang again, with their zany afterparties, decked out in neon wigs and '70s flares. One time they even dragged me off to the police station, asking the cop on duty if he'd seen John Travolta, taking photos of the interrogation, but the real action was in Europe. I'd started to build something and didn't want to be forgotten. If I wanted to make a career in music on a global level, it had to be in Europe, so Australia seemed irrelevant. Now I was more interested in experiencing new cultures, so Australia felt like the UK in the sun, however fun it was. I was there to spin some tunes, drink some tinnies, and skip the winter. After three months, I was back in England for the start of spring.

I signed on the dole the day I landed, looking bleakly at all the grim faces in the waiting room. I felt like I'd been beamed in from another galaxy; fun in the sun has that effect when it's done. I wanted the lifestyle all year, so I started putting on my Familia club nights in London with DJs I'd met: Tiefschwarz, James Zabiela, Nic Fanciulli, Lee Burridge, Konrad Black,

Steve Bug, Damian Lazarus, and many more came to play for me. This was pre-Facebook and Instagram, so I was out at nights with a bag of posters and flyers on my back. Again, I often ended up in the back of a police van, but I learnt what I could get away with, dodged the police, and the Familia parties became very successful.

I was starting to DJ on the next level now, playing gigs at some of the best clubs in London alongside top DJs. Soon Nic Fanciulli asked me to be his warm-up DJ and tour manager, which I could combine with my own DJing, and I was back on the road again. I remember one particularly gruelling weekend: Chicago, Toronto, Mexico City and Bogota in four nights with hardly any sleep. I landed at Heathrow, not knowing what day it was. The woman at passport control asked me where I'd flown in from, and I had no idea. I stood in front of her for about a minute, shaking my head. She was looking at me like I was a fool, but I was braindead from sleep deprivation, soon to become a common post-tour phenomenon.

I was starting to make decent money, so I moved out to Barcelona in May 2006 and ran the show from there. It had always been a dream of mine to live in Barna. The digital world was evolving, allowing remote working, and you no longer needed to be in the country where you made your business. All I needed was a Wi-Fi connection and an airport. I settled into Barcelona quickly; I already had some Ibiza friends there. I used to fly back to London for Familia, run the party, look after the guest DJ, play the final set, and fly back to Barcelona with the cash.

DJing, promoting and tour managing was becoming a full-time thing. I'd only really toured Europe before, but I started touring in North and South America, Asia, and Africa regularly as well as every country in Europe. I was making enough money to start paying back my student debt, but it was really hard touring. My bank called one day saying they believed my credit card details had been cloned; it had been used in Mexico, Colombia, the United States and Canada in the space of four days. "Actually, that was me making all of the transactions," I said, trying to explain how it was physically possible.

After arriving back home, it would often take forty-eight hours for my brain to function fully, so I stayed home alone, not speaking to anyone. It was a weird and wild way of living, something many friends and family didn't approve of or understand, but everything was moving steadily forward. It was exactly what I'd dreamed of: travelling the world, playing music, working with top artists, and meeting like-minded, global people.

Discovering Carnival Land

My newly improved bank balance allowed me to head to Rio and check out the carnival — a never-ending parade of musical flirtation. Splashes of colour, perfectly synced dancing, dinosaurs popping out of floats, booty-shaking carnival queens and hundreds of drummers. The bateria batucada drummers gave me goosebumps, and the sound vibrated through every cell of my body. I was there for thirteen hours and never got bored. The Samba schools spend the entire year rehearsing, so it's perfectly executed. Without doubt, it was the best event in the world I'd seen, and I'd been to a few.

But when I saw a flyer on the floor for Sasha playing at a club called Warung Beach Club, I texted him to see if it was worth flying down. "Man, it's one of the best clubs around; get your ass down here," he said. So half-way through the carnival, my friends and I left Rio and flew south to Itajaí. It was a very different vibe to Rio. Down in the south, the people all have European heritage with German and Italian surnames. Blue-eyed, beautiful boys and girls — it was clear why most of the Brazilian supermodels came from here — the mix of Europe and South America produced these perfect creatures. They spoke better English in the south than in the north, so I could communicate more and made a real connection with their welcoming smiles and penchant for enjoying life to the max. We had to watch our backs in Rio and São Paulo, but Itajaí felt as safe as Europe.

The main difference here was that instead of samba, the music was electronic. Warung totally blew me away, and I've been there every year since. Warung, to this day, remains my favourite club in the world. When that place goes off, there is nothing like it. It's a temple on the beach run by amazing people, the sun comes up in the morning over the sea and shines directly through the temple, making it all yellow and the mood changes from dark to light, the music policy is very cool, and some of the most beautiful people in the whole world party here.

Sasha rocked it just like he did at my first ever club night eleven years before, just with a slightly more spectacular setting than in Bristol. He played until noon, and everyone stayed — jammed in like sardines. That famous sunrise blasted through the club and created a whole new morning vibe; the sunglasses were out, and the mercury was creeping up and up. It was a Thursday night, but it was carnival time, and nobody was going anywhere. This was the ultimate party experience. Alessandra Ambrosio, the Victoria's Secret supermodel, came up to me and said, "Hey, how you doing?" and started a long conversation. Was I dreaming? No, it's just Brazil. Brazilians are very open, friendly and positive, quite similar to Aussies in that respect, and it was something that I became myself, as a result of spending time in both countries.

Brazil is, without doubt, one of the biggest party capitals in the world. The state of Santa Catarina, which includes Florianopolis, Camboriu and Itajaí, has more clubs than Ibiza. During carnival or special events like New Year's Eve, it's one of the best places to be on the planet.

Santa Catarina became my summer home every winter for six years — all because of Warung. I had spent several summers in Australia escaping the cold European winter, but why hadn't I thought of Brazil before? South America had been a dream of mine to tour for many years but little did I know it was the hotbed of electronic music. The idea I had of Brazil of a country full of dangerous slums, dodgy plastic surgery and kids playing football with tin cans on street corners was wide of the mark. Kind of.

DJs often take time off after New Year, and there are not many events, so with Carnival usually being in February, it was the perfect place to go — good weather, amazing people and a huge party scene, which was booming. It was ironic how the DJs and party people I met in Brazil longed to visit Europe to party there, but the parties in Brazil were so much better than what we had. I used to count down the days to go to Brazil, and every time was better than the previous. In the south, I used to be the only European person wherever I went, and the people were interested in meeting me. The United Kingdom can mean different things to different people. Here was a place where they liked the Brits, possibly because they never met any, so I had a clean slate, and I met some of the kindest, warmest (and craziest) people in the whole world. They never want to go home, which is the perfect ground for DJs.

The local DJs seemed to like me as much as my music, so I quickly gained a good friend base, and Santa Catarina became my home for a few months every winter. I had a crazy connection with Brazilians which I have never matched in any other country. I ended up living for one summer season with one of the top local DJs, Paulo Boghosian, who treated me like one of his own. He had a pimpin' summer home in Florianopolis. It was a wild summer that almost matched my Ibiza hedonism. Whenever my European DJ friends were in town, they would hit me up, and I would join them on tour, and it was wild — absolutely wild. I even started to feel like a Brazilian; my Portuguese was getting me by, and I started getting called "Rossinho".

I travelled all around the country, touring with several DJs, from the South to the Amazon jungle and several cities around Brazil that I had never heard of. I discovered great parties, culture, and the people were not just warm — they were red hot. I experienced that famous Latino blood that we read about. From Manaus in the Amazon rainforest to the German-influenced Porto Alegre, I was fascinated by this melting pot of mixed cultures. So many crazy things happened to me while in Brazil. I was carjacked in São Paulo, robbed on Ipanema beach in Rio, attempted to dance the samba at a school in Curitiba, but one weekend stands out in particular. I got booked to play at my favourite club, Warung, in 2009, which was a dream come true. I played for four hours — that special crowd jammed in like sardines fixated on the music. I was the last one out when the sun was rising.

Next day, we were off to D-Edge in São Paulo. It was the first club I ever went to in Brazil. Every wall is a throbbing lit-up graphic equaliser that pulsates in time to the beat. You can't stand still in there even if you tried — the visual experience would even move someone who couldn't hear. I'd been there so many times and never thought I would have the chance to play there, but here I was. It was the day before my birthday. When I'm in Brazil, I always make sure I have one churrascaria — the Brazilian steakhouses with unlimited meat on skewers. The gig in São Paulo, as always, went on until nine a.m., I slept a few hours, and the flight was at four p.m. the next day to a city called Ribeirão Preto. I woke up at midday and went to the churrascaria to treat myself for my birthday. I absolutely stuffed myself with the most delicious meat I could eat and waddled back to the hotel. These meals are so big that once you have one, you don't want to look at another one for a long time. I went to the airport and flew to Ribeirão Preto. The owners of the club met us at the airport, and somehow, they knew it was my birthday. When I came through arrivals, they said, "Happy Birthday! We have a surprise for you."

I was like, "Cool, thank you." And they drove us directly to... a churrascaria! I couldn't believe it. I was still completely full from the first one and couldn't even look at food, and here we were in another Brazilian steakhouse a few hours later. I ate a little, just to be polite. I was about to burst and then came another surprise — a huge birthday cake. I told them that I honestly couldn't eat any more and asked if I could take it to the hotel to eat later, so they put it in a box, and I took it with me. I had a nap, woke up and felt great and ready to play the party.

I arrived at the club and played for around three hours. The vibe was amazing; it was a very beautiful outdoor club and absolutely packed. There was a girl in the corner looking at me during my whole set, she looked nice, so when I finished playing, I went to speak to her. She spoke good English, so we hung out, and she was very cool. It got to six a.m., and the party was finishing, so the driver took me home, and she came with me. We were pretty drunk, stumbling around. I opened the door to my suite but couldn't find the switch for the lights. We started making out on the sofa, and things were getting quite steamy, but we couldn't really see what we were doing as it was so dark. The girl suddenly said, "Stop, wait. What's this?"

I said, "What's wrong?"

She replied, "I'm covered in something sticky."

I shone my phone light and realised that we had been making out on my birthday cake box, which was only made of that thin white card, and the cake had squashed through the gaps and was all over us — icing, jam, sponge, and everything else. It was also all over the sofa, walls, floor… talk about a moment killer. She went to the shower, and I tried to clean it up, but I was making it worse. We just went to sleep; the moment had well and truly gone.

Next day, I woke up to the smell of jam and cake and a huge hangover. I tried again to clean up the mess but decided to leave it to the experts. I left a note to the cleaner in Portuguese: "Sorry for the mess, but please enjoy the cake."

Brazilians have party engrained into them, the financial crisis has hurt them in recent years, so the scene is not as strong as it was before, but, for sure, it will be back one day to its best, and I can't wait to return, especially to Warung — the club we nickname "The Temple".

One + One = Three

In 2007 came the idea of two high-profile DJ friends of mine — James Zabiela and Nic Fanciulli to tour together, with me doubling up as the warm-up DJ and tour manager — the One + One tour. It started in May 2007 in the USA. The plan was to drive around the whole of America from Los Angeles to New York, doing twenty-one gigs in thirty nights. What could possibly go wrong?

James and Nic were two of my old friends — it was going to be fun, but we didn't know the obstacles that were going to hit us on the way. James had a wild idea that we should do the whole tour in an RV. It sounded a bit pointless to me, as we were staying in five-star hotels anyway, but James was set on this idea of doing it in a Scooby-Doo van. We landed a few days early in L.A. and went to pick up this RV.

"It'll be its maiden voyage," the whacked-out guy had told us on the phone.

I got to this shady yard in the back streets of the ghetto and found this rusty old RV, which was held together with glue. *Fuck, Nic isn't going to love this,* and *How is this going to make it to New York?* were the first thoughts that came to mind. The piece of shit was a liability.

I remember reversing out of the Roosevelt Car Park in Hollywood, not being able to see anything behind me. *Boomf!* That sound that everyone dreads. I got out and saw an orange Lamborghini on the corner of the van. My heart sank. Of all the things to hit, I'd found the Lambo. I got closer, and somehow, I had hit the hotel wall, which crashed down, and narrowly missed the Lambo. Someone was watching over me, maybe. Our RV was built like a tank and had no damage at all. I gave my name and details to the Roosevelt staff, and they told me that they would be in touch so I could pay for the wall damage, but I never heard from them. We persuaded James that this was not going to get us around the USA — it wasn't the Scooby-Doo van that he had told to his fans, but, eventually, he saw sense. We ditched it, and we were away in a brand-new SUV with working lights and everything.

The USA is the best country for touring. The people are so welcoming, the roads are good, it's mostly safe, and most of the clubs close at two a.m. — very early compared to Europe. So even if you are on a twenty-one-date tour, you have the option to be in bed by two thirty in most places, fresh for the long drive the next day. Some of the drives were a killer fourteen hours. The difference from state to state is vast. Considering the number of miles we did, the incidents were minimal, but one could have been ugly. We were coming into

Albuquerque, and two shady-looking guys in another SUV were acting like something from *Boyz n the Hood* trying to block me from exiting the highway. My Newport instinct kicked in, and I showed them the middle finger and sped up in front of them to exit off the ramp. Thirty seconds later, they pulled up right next to us, holding guns through the window at our faces. I put my foot down and started racing away from them, and they pursued. I was driving with my head ducked down, running through red lights, over the sidewalks, trying to lose them somehow, but they kept following us. James was dialling 911 and showing them his phone through the window, but that didn't stop them tearing after us. The pursuit seemed to go on forever. Nic was screaming at me, "You're not back in Wales now; this is real gangland!" Except with toy guns.

James managed to look closely and saw that their guns were not real, so I slowed down, gave them an apologetic wave, and they let us go. A real taste of American gangland. Perhaps a lucky escape, or just naïvety. We lived to tell the tale. Suddenly my phone was ringing. "Where are you guys?" It was the promoter. We had driven over a time zone and lost one hour, and the club was opening in forty-five minutes. I put my foot down again, this time with my head up, looking where I was going. We arrived in Albuquerque; I dropped JZ and Nic at the hotel and was bang on time for doors-open. Not easy to play after that episode, but a few vodkas later, I was into the groove.

The crazy capers didn't stop there. Next day, I was driving over the state border from New Mexico to Colorado. The speed limit cunningly drops from seventy-five miles per hour to sixty-five, and, of course, there was a cop waiting right on the border — easy winnings for him. I saw the blue light in my mirror and the sound of a siren that I had not heard since watching *Smokey and the Bandit*. I was trying to find a spot to pull over, but there was nowhere to stop. I slowed down, continued to drive with my hazard lights on, looking for somewhere to pull over, but there was nowhere. The cop was right up next to me with his megaphone. It was like a scene out of *The Dukes of Hazzard*, he yelled at me to stop, so I just stopped where I was on the highway. "Put your hands up!" he screamed. I thought that I might hear that phrase a few times on this tour but not exactly in this situation. He had me over the car with my hands up. I tried to explain to him that I had tried to find a safe place to pull over, but he didn't even understand my accent. They say that ninety per cent of Americans have never left the USA; I doubt if this guy had ever even crossed the border that I had just driven over. He asked where I lived.

"London," I said.

"London, Ontario?"

Jesus — this was new territory. He told me that he had already called a pursuit. If I hadn't stopped the car at that moment, there would have been up to ten cop cars and a helicopter chasing me. A little extreme, I thought, and after I had answered a few more of his overzealous questions with him pushing his gun into my back, he realised that he had overreacted and cancelled the pursuit and backup. He wrote me a citation, and I was on my way, much more wary of state border lines and over-zealous sergeant major US cops who had probably been bullied at school. I had seen first-hand the famous trigger-happy American cops and the needless problems they cause.

The next few days were relatively *calm*. Now we were in the mid-states, and people were notably different. Most were very welcoming, but some were strange on a different level from anything I had seen before. I was filling up with gas in a remote gas station in Kansas on a dark night, James and Nic were sleeping. A scary-looking woman next to me was filling up her car and had a T-shirt with "Jesus Is Alive" on the front. She was staring at me with a sinister look. It was like a scene from *The Texas Chain Saw Massacre.* I was filling up as quickly as possible, but she approached me and said, "Hey, do you believe in Jesus?"

I politely said, "Hey, sorry, I'm in a rush right now." But she wouldn't stop.

She followed me into the store, saying, "You must believe in Jesus! He's around us; can you feel him?"

I scurried away, back into the car, and she followed me, shouting through the window that I had to come to her church on Sunday and meet Jesus. I sped away and got out of Kansas as quickly as I could, fearing that I was going to be lured into some cult.

We had planned to split the driving, but I drove the whole way around. I preferred it. I can't sleep in anything except a bed anyway. So many interesting places: San Francisco, New Orleans (post-Hurricane Katrina), Scottsdale, Austin, Tampa, Miami, D.C., and New York were the standout gigs, but considering the nature of the road trip, the ravers came out on all days of the week, rain or shine, with that famous welcoming American spirit. The smaller or more remote the town, the more appreciative the people are. I picked up their positivity immediately. Their cup is always half-full. They genuinely want the best for you. I hadn't experienced this before in Europe. I was used to people being bitter, twisted, and negative (me included). Here they look on the bright side. Americans will never tell you that they've had a shit night, even if it was the worst night ever.

The USA made me a much better person. Much more positive and open. A lot of crazy shit happened to us when we were there, but there was always someone on hand to help; nobody walked away from us. It's by no means perfect, but if you take the positives, it's an amazing country. The One + One USA tour was the best month of my life, and I knew it. I took it all in despite the ups and downs, the sleep deprivation, and the low energy levels; I lapped up every minute.

Japanophile

Japan. My favourite country in the world. The One +
One tour took me there for the first time in 2008. Yes, I
am undoubtedly a Japanophile. Entering Tokyo for the
first time, it hits you. The noise, the neon, the
hecticness, the businessmen with perfectly tailored suits
bowing to each other for two minutes on the street, the
smells, the flashing lights, the vending machines selling
schoolgirls' worn clothes; weird, warped, but
fascinating. It's Times Square multiplied by a thousand.

The promoter, Yuuki, picked us up from the airport.
I had heard so much about Womb. It was every DJ's
favourite club, and this was the big one of the tour, the
one we had been counting down to. I had watched so
many videos; it felt like I had been there before. I
walked in before opening time, and there it was — a
futuristic emporium, wall-to-wall visuals, massive
speaker stacks that pounded so hard that I almost
regurgitated my sashimi.

I was more nervous than ever before. I walked into
the famous DJ booth: a futuristic cockpit of technology,
pitch black but glowing with a thousand flashing
gauges. I opened my bag and saw not my music, but my
shoes. Not a good start. Luckily, the Japanese will never

say no, and within a few minutes, my real bag of music was in the club with me. No idea how they got it from my room.

I started playing slow and quiet, but within minutes, the whole place was shuddering. How was that possible? These were warm-up tracks that I had played on the whole tour, foot-tappers that you play when the crowd trickle in. Building up the night was a skill that I had learnt from years as a warm-up DJ. Teasing them with foreplay, choosing when to fill the dance floor with carefully selected grooves, moving through the gears step by step. But this was Japan. They were not messing around. One by one, they came in and took their positions at the front. There were no drinks in sight, just hundreds of excited, hyperactive, ecstatic faces fixated on me, dancing like crazy to 118 beats per minute tracks that were made to be listened to in your armchair. I was feeling guilty. The opening DJ should never wear a crowd out too early; it's an unwritten rule. But what could I do? Whatever I played, they danced, shouted, and screamed like it was peak time. After one hour, the dance floor was full. Nic texted me, asking how it was going. I told him, almost apologetically, that it was rocking already. "Just go for it," he replied. "You can't hold them back in Tokyo."

It was not even midnight, and we had reached ecstatic levels. I had never seen people so appreciative and eccentric before. The sound was ripping through the club, my drink was walking along the booth, my CDs were falling out of their sleeves. I heard a huge roar. Had Elvis just entered the building? No, it was James and Nic. It was the point when the crowd reached fever pitch, and I took it up another notch, and they went wilder than before. Yuuki turned to me and said, "Ross, you are crying."

Yes, I had tears in my eyes. The occasion was overwhelming. I had fallen in love with Japan, its people, its food, and its deep culture.

Japanese are polite, disciplined, and respectful. The respect that they have for others is what I noticed above everything else. All of the values that so many cultures seem to have forgotten in the last few decades are still strong in Japan. If you see anyone behaving badly, you can guarantee that they will be foreign. The culture can be strange, bordering on twisted sometimes, but fascinating, engrossing and enchanting. I was hooked from my first trip, and I have been every year since — I can't get enough.

My phone has a list of my favourite restaurants for almost every city in the world. To my friends, I'm the unofficial Tripadvisor; but for Tokyo, there is no need for a list. Every restaurant is good; the Japanese don't do anything badly. Almost every building in Shibuya, Shinjuku, Roppongi has restaurants stacked on top of each other; you could go to a new restaurant every day for thirty years.

One thing I noticed in Japan is the number of people who casually take naps in public. This is a massively overworked nation. Waking up at five a.m., getting stuffed into a crammed train, packed in like sardines by a "train pusher" with white gloves, then working continuously for ten hours is a standard day. It's not unusual to see a businessman sleeping on the street in the evening with his briefcase and laptop beside him on the ground. *What if he gets robbed?* was my first thought when I saw it. It wouldn't happen in Japan. It's his property, so nobody else will touch it. This is ultimate respect. I've seen Japanese wake up from a casual street nap, dust themselves off and continue their evening as if it's totally normal. It's weirdly fascinating. I've walked into a burger restaurant at five a.m., and every single person was slumped in their seat, eyes shut, heads almost touching their empty food wrappers. Were the burgers off? Had someone gassed the joint? It was eerie. I sat down and cautiously ate mine, watching the people around me, wondering if I should check their pulses. One by one, they slowly woke up and walked out to take the first train home. Fantastically bizarre.

Many Japanese live far out of town in small apartments, so they don't socialise at home. Drinking after work is the norm. If they miss the last train, an expensive taxi is not even an option. Neither is cooking at home in a tiny kitchen. Why would you when there is so much amazing food around? They spend the least amount of time at home as possible, and this has created their nap culture.

I always make friends with the locals wherever I am. Why do some people only have friends from their own country? How boring. There is so much to learn from people from around the world, but some nations are difficult to break down. The language barrier in Japan is a huge hurdle. My Japanese goes as far as *kanpai* (you get to know *cheers* in every language in this job). Most learn English at school, but they rarely get to practice, and they are famously a nation of perfectionists. This can be frustrating when you feel that they understand you, but they are too shy to reply. When you meet the ones who are confident to speak English, that's when you make the connections.

I've had some wild tours in Japan. From the moment I arrive at Narita Airport until the moment I leave, I don't ever check the news or social network sites to see the world outside the Japan bubble. It's a parallel universe. A place where we let ourselves go. My favourite drink is saké. Nothing else gets me so happily drunk. When we drink saké in Japan, crazy things happen. The coolest of hipster DJs, who are never usually seen listening to anything other than minimal techno, will burst into Whitney Houston in private karaoke, dancing on tables, playing air guitar, letting themselves go like they can't do anywhere else — always saké fuelled.

It was late April 2012, and my sixth tour of Japan. The club this time was Vision. Another futuristic cauldron of sound and lighting. It was a warm spring evening, and I was touring with a DJ who had a big following in Japan. I entered the particularly dark DJ booth and placed my bag in the corner. The club quickly filled up — it was the afterparty of Hacienda Oiso, and the festival crowd had arrived at the same time. Many friends were in town; the saké was flowing. This was a proper party, but the DJ booth was uncomfortably hot. How was a club so famous for its hi-tech technology so cool on the dance floor but so hot in the booth? "Ross, I'm so hot. I don't think I can continue like this," the DJ said to me.

I asked the technician if he could turn up the air-con.

"It's already on full," his Google translator message said, scared to tell me incorrect information.

"If I'm gonna continue, I need to take my clothes off," said the DJ. I thought he was joking, but off they came with the exception of his boxers — thank God — the Japanese are even more prudish than the British. I saw a sea of shocked-looking faces from the locals and some smiles from the expats. The energy went up another level; people love to see a DJ enjoying himself, and they feed off that energy. The idea of doing it myself entered my head for a moment, so intense was the heat, but I decided against it. I had already made three girls scream earlier in the evening by walking into the girls' toilets by mistake. I had to bow apologetically with my hands up while reversing out. Not the best country to be making mistakes like that. Two hours after the clothes came off, the lights went up, and the music stopped. I picked up my bag and saw a small vent behind where it had been sitting. Shit. My bag had been blocking the air-con for the DJ booth. It was all my fault for the sweltering heat that forced the DJ to play half-naked for most of the night. I managed to keep that one quiet. He was having a great time anyway.

We decided to walk to the hotel. I guess the DJ found it liberating, and his clothes never went back on. This was the Japanese parallel universe. Walking through Shibuya at five a.m. with a half-naked DJ, three drunk promoters and four Russian models was a sight to behold. Imagine doing this in the centre of Frankfurt? The saké made everything seem normal. The receptionists at Cerulean Tower gasped while somehow maintaining their bowing tradition. The lift doors opened, and I heard a high-pitched shriek. A glamourous, perfectly dressed Japanese couple walked out, hands over their mouths. They were the first ones down for breakfast and didn't expect to see a sight like us. The room service waiter was kept on his toes up and down to my room on the twenty-sixth floor that morning. He should be writing his own book of stories of when DJs are in town. I remember seeing the sun high in the sky over Mount Fuji before finally passing out. The check-out bill was another story.

Despite my Western-style exploits, Japan is a place where the culture encourages me back every time. The culture of respect and politeness is both reforming and humbling. I always return from Japan a better person than when I arrived. Tokyo, in particular, is a melting pot of cultures, but the strong Japanese culture rises over the others. The music scene has taken a dip in recent years, partly because of Japan's population collapse. The workaholic culture has meant a sharp drop in birth rates and, therefore, fewer young people. The burnt-out workers are too busy to make babies, and many are even having stress-free virtual relationships. Maybe they are on to something.

Zero to Hero

Back to 2008, and the One + One tour was over. I'd had my big break — now it was up to me to kick on. I was jumping up and down on my bed when I got the call from a big DJ agency who told me that they wanted to sign me, and I would be opening for Deep Dish on tour. Life-changing. But my dream was all over before it began when the duo suddenly broke up, and the global financial crisis crashed the music industry with the same brutality that Covid did twelve years later.

Gig activity was down for everyone; it was not the time to be looking for gigs now. The only way to break through now was by making my own tracks. I found some studios in Barcelona, but the owners either didn't show up or were hours late. I saw the warning flags and moved back to London. Now was not the time to be relying on lazy people. I'm not a big fan of London, but at least people get things done there.

I found a London studio with an engineer, and we made an eleven-track album, *Zero to Hero*. Digital record stores and file sharing sites were replacing the old way of buying physical music. Now you could effectively make a track on one day and have it played by DJs in another country that night, and that's exactly what happened. I sent a test track to James Zabiela, who was on tour in Peru the day I finished it. I woke up next morning, and in my inbox was a video from James, who had played it at a huge festival in Lima. It was the boost that I needed. The road test had worked, the album was released a few months later, and it was soon being played by many of the big DJs from Laurent Garnier to John Digweed. Most of the tracks were high on the Beatport Charts, and many of the big DJs were playing them. The album was a surprise success, and I started to be booked more often, despite the crisis.

These were still the early days of Facebook and Instagram, and Twitter didn't yet exist. Music production was the best way to promote yourself. It was no longer enough just to send out a DJ mix to promoters and hope they liked it. The bar had been raised massively now. There were too many good DJs around, and anyone with an internet connection had access to most music. It was the first profession where if you wanted to be successful in one job — a DJ — you had to be good at another: producing music.

Despite the financial crash, I started to do my own tours in many countries: Latvia, Germany, Lithuania, France, Italy, and Switzerland were the first places I went, and the rest of the weekends, there was always one DJ who asked me to tour with him. So, I was constantly out there touring every weekend and spent most of the weekdays recovering. The more you play, the better a DJ you become, and the more you tour, the wiser you become at that too. Touring with the big DJs also teaches you many things, as you can watch what they do, how they play, how they work the crowd. You can learn from their mistakes too. Some of the current big DJs started out as tour managers for other DJs, which is how they made their connections and learnt their trade.

I released over one hundred tracks; some of them did very well. In the UK, we grew up religiously listening to Pete Tong on BBC Radio 1 on a Friday evening. Whatever he played became big, so everyone wanted Pete to play their tunes. I remember driving down the King's Road in London one Friday evening on a warm summer's night listening to Pete when suddenly he played my track. I totally lost my concentration. I had to pull over and sit there, taking it all in. It later became a regular thing; I used to be disappointed on weeks when he didn't play one of mine.

I was still quite young and making my own decisions, and without good guidance, I made a lot of mistakes. One major mistake was releasing the tracks myself on my own newly formed label rather than sending them to the established labels. Releasing them on the big labels would have given me a bigger profile. The market is so saturated with DJs and labels that new artists releasing on new labels mostly go under the radar, however good the music is. Even though my album did well, it would have done even better had it been released on a big established label. Eventually, I started to realise that it's better to give tracks to the big labels for them to release.

Another common mistake that I used to make was finishing a day in the studio and thinking that I had a big track ready to go. I was eager to play the track to everyone, so I would send it out immediately to DJs and labels, then the next day listen again with fresh ears and realise that it needed more work. I was getting too excited. When you have to send a second version of a track to someone, they can easily just switch off from you. I should have been more patient. One extra day is not long to wait to get something perfect.

Years ago, all you needed was to be a good DJ, and you would likely get a career with the right contacts and getting the upfront vinyl before anyone else. Then came the digital age, and online music stores meant that everyone had access to the same music, which resulted in thousands more DJs, so a new mark had to be set: producing good tracks. I had worked out the formula. I had a long way to go, but for now, I was living the dream.

The Baltic Dream Turns Sour

I started to play in Latvia. I was regularly going to the Baltics, and my fanbase there was growing. Then my agent received a call from the top promoter and DJ in neighbouring Lithuania — Ignas — who booked me to play at Pacha Vilnius. I remember the date so clearly: 4 January 2008. *Who goes out on 4 January in minus twenty degrees Celsius temperatures?* I remember thinking. Especially, to see me play; surely nobody knew me? I had never been to Lithuania before and couldn't even tell you where it was on a map. The weeks after New Year are typically quiet in most places around the world, especially in the cold Northern Hemisphere. Most people are skint after the holidays or just don't have the energy. I wasn't sure if I should accept the gig, but I was talked into it by my agent. I flew into Vilnius. It was dark, freezing cold and very depressing. The old Soviet-style buildings were grey, run-down and decrepit. There was hardly any movement in the streets, even on a Friday evening. I didn't have any expectations for the party. For sure, it would be bad. We drove through the miserable streets, not seeing a soul, but at the end of the road, I saw a glow getting brighter as we approached. It was a brand-new lit-up building, smart and modern. It looked totally out of place among the shabby old Stalinist buildings around it. It was the entrance to Pacha. I recognised those famous Pacha cherries, and suddenly I started to get a good feeling. The party people were lining up right down the street in freezing temperatures. I recognised a few of them from Latvia; they had travelled to see me.

I walked into the club, and it was a different world. The venue was typically Pacha — glamorous and elegant. The people were beautiful; the girls far outnumbered the guys. It was hard to believe this was the same depressing city I had been driving through a few minutes before. Clearly Lithuanians didn't go so crazy for Christmas and New Year as we do in the UK, where nobody has any money left by 2 January. I took my place in the booth, and people started to fill the dance floor even before I had played my first track. Ignas said, "Look, they know you."

I was like, "How? I haven't been here before."

"I've been pushing your music here for months," he replied. Ignas was not only the biggest DJ in Lithuania, but his radio show was the Lithuanian equivalent of *Pete Tong's Essential Selection*. Ignas had been supporting my music on his show, and people had got to know me. The power of the internet was starting to be evident now. Facebook was still in its infancy, Instagram still didn't exist, but access to information was getting easier for people, and DJs could exploit it. The night was a huge success; Ignas invited me back to play again and again in several different venues around Lithuania. It was becoming a second home.

One year after my debut in Lithuania, I was booked to play at another club — Exit in Kaunas. I had played there a few times already; it was a boring city, even more grey than Vilnius, but Exit was the shining light. For me, it was one of the best clubs in Europe. The crowd were always super hyperactive, and they loved the music. I had built up a connection with them better than anywhere else I was playing at the time. That weekend I was playing Ljubljana on the Friday and Kaunas on the Saturday. I used to love a Central/Eastern European weekend. My old friend from university, Mancub, had heard my stories and decided to come with me. It was his first time in Lithuania. He wanted to see Vilnius, so we stayed until the Monday so that we could go out in Vilnius on the Sunday night. Now, what we didn't think of was that on a Sunday night in the middle of winter during a financial crisis, Vilnius isn't exactly rocking. We went for dinner and to a few bars, but everywhere was dead, so we gave up and went back to the pizza restaurant where we had started.

We sat there having one final drink before going home when one of the three girls who were sitting at the table next to us said, "Hey guys, what are you doing tonight?"

We told her that we had tried a few places and everywhere was dead, so we were going home.

She said, "We know a great party tonight; you can come with us."

We looked at each other and thought, OK, nothing to lose. What could possibly go wrong? We jumped in a taxi with them and went to a club. We entered the club but again, there was no-one inside except one moody looking dragon behind the bar. I said to the girls, "Where are all the people?"

"The people will come," they promised. "We are just a bit early."

At that point, the alarm bells should have rung, as it was already midnight on a Sunday night. We were naïve and didn't see what was coming.

"OK, we will stay for one drink and see," I replied, so I went to the bar and ordered our drinks and told the girls to tell the woman what they wanted.

She said, "Take a seat. I will bring the drinks over."

We sat down with the girls for a while, but nobody else arrived in the club. I said to my friend eventually, "Let's go; this is boring." I asked for the bill. Dragon-woman brought the bill over to us. I had to look twice. The total was an insane amount for a few drinks. She stood there with the credit card machine.

I told her that it was not right, but she pointed to the menu, which was all normal-priced drinks apart from the one hidden *scam* drink which the girls had ordered. We slowly realised that we had been conned. Suddenly, two huge Russian security guards appeared from nowhere and blocked the door so that we couldn't get out. I tried to call the owner of the club I had played at, but my phone battery was dead. We were stuck.

The bill was around €2,000 for a few short drinks. The girls were claiming to have nothing to do with the scam, crying their eyes out with crocodile tears. I was arguing with the security, refusing to pay for the girls' scam drinks. I had heard stories about guys who go to dodgy strip clubs in Eastern European countries being scammed in a similar way, but this was not a strip club; it was a normal bar (as we thought). This bar was operating the same kind of scam, sending girls out into the city to find unsuspecting tourist guys to bring to the club and rob.

We argued for almost two hours, but the security started to be aggressive, pushing me around, stealing my leather jacket and sunglasses, even trying them on in front of me before pushing us around. The girls offered to pay half of the amount. They even did a transaction in the card machine. Mancub snatched the receipt out of the machine, which read: "Void transaction." If there was any doubt in our minds that we were getting scammed, it was now confirmed. We argued some more, but they wouldn't let us go without paying the €2K. We finally gave in. Mancub gave his credit card, which the dragon-woman swiftly swiped while she had the chance, and they finally let us go.

As we walked out of the door, the girls' crying instantly stopped. It wasn't an Oscar performance, but it was an easy night's work. I could imagine our money getting split between the girls, the security guards, and the dragon. Someone had a nice new jacket and sunglasses.

Next morning, we called Ignas, who called the police, who said they could do nothing. The scam didn't break any laws, and ironically it was the only bar in Vilnius that made any money that night. Very clever and a big lesson learnt: Never go to bars that haven't been recommended, and definitely don't go with people you know nothing about.

These days with dating apps, these scams are even more rife; I have friends who have been robbed in similar ways for much higher sums. This was a classic set-up, and we had been done.

Next morning, before the airport, we tried to use our leftover cash to pay for breakfast. The cash which the taxi driver had given us in change after we left the scam club. "These are Russian rubles. They have no worth," the waitress said. Scammed again.

I couldn't wait to get out of the country. Nothing makes you feel lower than getting robbed. I had so many questions. How could these girls live a life like that? How could dragon-woman sleep at night? How did my leather jacket fit such a huge bouncer? Desperate times call for desperate measures, I guess. The financial crash had hit many people hard. Many bars in Eastern Europe had turned to these scams as they couldn't make a living with normal trade, so they resorted to this. Smart and sinister at the same time.

It took me a long time until I was ready to go back to Lithuania; the incident left a bad taste in my mouth. I was scared to go, but I still kept my connections with the fans. It even made the news. Many contacted me with apologetic messages; some offered me protection if I came back. I'm sure they were joking, but it was nice for people to reach out.

Nine months later, I returned, and what a welcome. They had made a special effort this time. It was Halloween, the biggest night of the year at Exit. Everyone had dressed up, and they were going crazy. It was a great few days, with good people. My faith in the country was restored. I never went back to that pizza restaurant again or spoke to anyone random, and I definitely didn't go looking for parties on a Sunday night.

Vilnius eventually became my second home. I got an apartment in the cosy Old Town, which became my Baltic base. Who would have thought? I used to spend my summer days off at the beautiful Baltic Sea. The resorts of Nida and Palanga are hidden gems in Europe. You can feel the magic there on those long summer nights. I would never have discovered them if it wasn't for Exit. Finally, the memories of that scam club eventually disappeared.

I learnt a lot about myself from living in Lithuania — somewhere so different from my own culture. People in the Baltics are notoriously cold and closed; it's very difficult to make friends. I had to learn quickly how to open them up, but I found it tough. When you are touring as a DJ, everyone wants to know you; it's easy. This was the other extreme. People constantly asked, "Why are you here?" with suspicious eyes. The men, especially, worried that you were coming to steal their women. The Soviet occupation for so many decades left its mark; the distrusting culture was still evident, even decades later.

The financial crash eventually took its toll on the Baltic club scene. One by one, the clubs closed down until there were just a few small ones, no bigger than the average bar. The cocktail bars with free entry took over. My many years spent travelling to both Latvia and Lithuania building up my fanbase all came to nothing. In terms of nightlife, the Baltics are a strange one. In every country in Europe, people like going out to clubs and dancing. Here, clubs just died away. I noticed a big change. People were not into music as they were before. I was keeping quiet during the week and counting down to the weekends.

Travelling on tour every weekend was tough. I used to joke that Vilnius doesn't fly anywhere direct, which is almost true. I spent my Friday and Sunday afternoons in Frankfurt Airport Business Lounge, often bumping into other DJs who also lived in remote places.

The freezing winters definitely put hairs on my chest. I learnt that below minus ten degrees Celsius, I don't function any more. Many of the locals hibernate for the winter, like bears, resurfacing in April when the snow stops falling. When the bars and restaurants start building their summer terraces, the mood lifts, and suddenly, the Old Town is buzzing. People start to open up. This is when you see the best of Lithuania. I had a mixed time there — lots of ups and downs. The cultural differences between Western and Eastern Europe are bigger than I thought. I'm an open person, but it doesn't work there. It was the first time I experienced people who didn't take to me. I hit a wall. There was no real expat scene. It was a big gamble to move there alone to such a different culture. Nothing ventured, nothing gained. I was glad I tried it, but I was off for new adventures.

A Spicy Mexican

Mexico City was high on my radar. I had heard great things. I've always loved Mexicans: warm-hearted people, cool and calm (the cartels aside). Their food is one of my favourites and, without doubt, it's one of the best party nations in the world. Every time I check Facebook to see where my fans are located, Mexico is always number one.

My first time in Mexico City, I was on tour with Danny Howells, Dubfire and Nic Fanciulli. We had all just landed in Mexico and were looking for a big feed. The W Hotel has a great restaurant, but we wanted the real Mexican taco experience. The hotel staff recommended a simple *cantina* next door, so off we went — four hungry DJs in Mexico City. Once again, what could go wrong?

We ordered all the tacos on the menu, numerous amounts of every dish, which was far more than four people should order. The waiter placed four different colour sauces on the table. "Be careful with these two," he said. "They are very spicy." The advice fell on deaf ears; we were deep in conversation and not really listening. The dishes arrived. I have never tasted tacos so good. I had eaten Mexican around the world before, but this was the real deal. I started with the mild yellow spice first, then onto the red, brown, and finally the green. This was the one that the waiter had particularly warned us about. When a Mexican warns you about a spice being dangerous, you should listen and take note. It definitely had a kick, but it didn't seem overly spicy to me. I continued eating the remaining tacos with the other guys; we even ordered more, all watered down with my favourite Mexican beer — Pacifico. Finally, we finished up, absolutely stuffed, and like four *gorditos*, we waddled back to the W for a quick disco nap before the party. It was at this point, when I finally walked into my room, that I realised that it was not your average hotel. The rooms were totally open plan. The bathroom and bedroom had no divide at all — everything was one room. It was a weird design, totally unconventional — a classic example of trying to be too clever. I was so glad I was staying alone.

My alarm went off after the usual ninety minutes, and we left for the club. Roots Magic Club was an apt name for it. It was an immense venue, huge visual screens everywhere, absolutely packed with up-for-it, cool party people. I was expecting something special, but this was even better than I imagined. It got to three a.m., and the mezcal was flowing. We had flown in from London that day, a sixteen-hour journey, but jetlag doesn't enter your mind when the party was that good.

Half-way through the night, a girl wandered into the DJ booth. How's this for a Mexican cliché: she had a tiny Chihuahua in her handbag. *Surely, he shouldn't be in here with this loud music?* I asked her why she had the dog in the club.

"Everywhere I go, the dog goes with me," she replied. She sounded like a girl who knew exactly what she wanted and always got it. After all, she had got into the DJ booth totally unchallenged by security who looked as scary as El Chapo's henchmen. I spoke to her for a while, and she was actually cool. I continued talking to her, not many other choices when you are stood on the stage, totally segregated from the crowd.

Five a.m. came, and the night was over. She asked me where we were all going. After partying was off the cards tonight as it was the first night of the tour. We had a gig in Monterrey the next day, so none of us wanted to continue, but she said that she would drive me to my hotel as she lived near the W. The other guys were laughing at me when I disappeared off with a random girl and a Chihuahua and the last bottle of mezcal in my hand. "I'll see you back at the hotel."

I got in her car, which she had brazenly parked right outside the door of the club — spaces usually reserved for the owner's Lamborghini. It was a dirty old Chevrolet. Clothes and shoes all over the seats. I had the Chihuahua in my lap; it was like a mouse, menacingly scurrying up to my face and down again. After my Lithuanian adventure a few months before, thoughts entered my mind that I could get robbed, be abandoned in a ditch, or have my mezcal stolen. I held onto the dog like it was my insurance. Who would rob a guy holding a puppy?

She invited herself (and the dog) into the hotel. She didn't comment on the strange design of the room; I guess she had seen it before. Suspiciously, most of these DJ groupies know all the hotels in town. We were just hanging out, listening to music, watching the dog scamper around the room. She dialled room service: a full European breakfast; she didn't even ask me if it was OK. It was then that I suddenly felt a sudden sharp pain in my stomach. It was like someone had put a knife into me. I leaned forward on the bed, my eyes closed. My stomach rumbled and churned, then the cramps came. I had totally forgotten about dinner before the club, but now the chillies were having their own afterparty.

The pain was excruciating. I got up to go to the bathroom, still leaning over. I couldn't stand up straight. Now I had a problem: no door, no divide, no wall, not even a curtain. With an audience of a girl and a dog, I was in trouble, and in a situation you would never want to be in.

I sat down on the toilet in full view of the bed. It was like a thunderbolt travelling through my body. For sure, it was the green one that the waiter had warned us about. Why hadn't I listened? How can a sauce be so deadly? Were the other guys experiencing the same? All was fine when I ate it; I love spicy food. I'd never had problems before. I didn't have problems in the club, but now this was punishment. I was sweating, overheating, glued to the toilet with one-metre flames firing out of my ass — all in front of this girl and the Chihuahua. She was pretending not to look at me, reading the W Hotel magazine. I'm sure it wasn't as interesting as the show going on in front of her. Just when I thought it couldn't get any worse, there was a knock at the door.

"Room service!"

You gotta be kidding me. I wanted the earth to swallow me up. Kill me now, please. She got up and answered the door. In came a tuxedoed waiter, his silver trolley rattling with cloches and fine dining plates. He folded the trolley out and set the breakfast trays on the bed right in front of me, the overprotective dog yapping around his ankles. I was still shooting fireworks, my face as white as the tablecloth.

I still couldn't stand up. If anything, I was getting worse. The waiter could blatantly see me but pretended that all was fine. He finished serving the breakfast. Blimey, she had ordered a banquet. "Enjoy your meal," he said.

Gracias, amigo! Now came the best part. He needed a signature for the room service. She didn't offer to sign it; the waiter brought it to me. I didn't even look at the amount; I was in no mood for currency calculations. I just signed and returned it. I just wanted this nightmare to be over. The dog chased him out of the door before running back and leaping on the bed, staring at his master, ready for some scraps of food.

"Are you OK?" the girl asked. "I'm hungry. Do you mind if I go ahead?"

After twenty more gruelling minutes, my stomach calmed down. The spice had passed through my body, ripping my digestive system to bits, but finally, I was in the clear. I made it to the shower, which was also in full view of the bed, but I was past the point of caring. I had a feeling of elation; it was almost like I was coming up on MDMA. Finally, I was able to stand up straight again.

I put on the dressing gown, and I lay down on the bed. I had no idea what to say. I had just made a total fool of myself right in front of a random stranger. She offered me some breakfast, but my appetite was gone. I poured some mezcal and sat back. I had a flight in four hours.

I was dozing off when suddenly I woke to hear someone talking loudly in Spanish. It was the girl talking on my hotel room phone. What was she doing? She started to cry. I couldn't understand a word of what she was saying. Finally, the phone call ended after thirty minutes. "Who was that?" I asked.

"It was my boyfriend," she replied.

"Calling you on my hotel phone?"

She had told her boyfriend to call her on the hotel phone as she had no credit left. It turned out that earlier in the night, she'd had a fight with him and went out alone. I guess now she'd started to miss him. The night was getting weirder and weirder. I told her that I had to go in a few hours, but she didn't want to leave, even asking me if she could come to Monterrey with us. We both fell asleep. I was dreaming that her narco-boyfriend was busting down my door when my alarm woke me up. The usual "guess where I am" game that I play when I wake up in a hotel room was an easy one. I had a Chihuahua in my face and the place stunk of eggs — the half-eaten food still on trays surrounding the bed. The girl didn't wake up; neither did the dog. I left them sleeping and met the guys down in the lobby who couldn't wait for my story. "Why does it always happen to you?" was the consensus yet again. I saw Kanye West in the lobby when I was leaving. I wondered what he thought of the weird rooms.

I returned to Mexico City two years later and was back in the W hotel. "Is there no other option?" I asked the promoter. Not this time. I was dreading going back, but on arrival, there was good news. The hotel had been modified, and the rooms redesigned to a more conventional style — separate bathrooms and everything. I wondered if the same thing had happened to anyone else or if they'd just had too many complaints. I stayed away from the green sauce that time, just to make sure.

Mexico is still one of my favourite countries in the world; the people are, without doubt, my favourite nation. Yes, it has its dangers — often we have armed guards escorting us to gigs — DJs are perfect kidnapping targets — but I never had any problems. It's the most welcoming, beautiful country, with a rich history, the coolest people, and the hottest chillies.

A White Christmas in Romania

It was mid-December 2010, and most of Europe was blanketed in snow. I was trudging through the old town of Riga. It was really feeling like Christmas. Next morning, we had a long journey to Galati in Romania. Galati is a small town near the border of Moldova and Ukraine, the absolute corner of Europe — three hours' drive from Bucharest on a good day, but Romanian parties are usually worth the effort. It was hard snowfall in Europe. I watched out of the plane window all the way from Riga to Bucharest and saw nothing but white the whole way. I've had some amazing nights in Romania; it's home to some of the best electronic parties in the world. This, however, was a total disaster.

Our flight was circling Bucharest for ages while the captain was asking for permission to land. The snow was so thick that they had to clear the runway again, especially for us. It was a sigh of relief when we finally touched down, but when we came out of arrivals, there was no-one to meet us.

I called the promoter. "Ross," he said, "listen! They've just closed the highway; the snowfall is so bad. But the party is going ahead. I'm getting you a Hummer to get through the village roads, just wait a bit longer, and the driver will be there."

I asked him if he thought this car would make it, and he assured me that all would be OK. We sat in McDonald's waiting; it was our first and only meal of the day — a typical day on tour. The H2 pulled up. The driver seemed excited to be driving a Hummer for the first time. "This truck can drive through anything," he said.

"How long will it take?" I asked him.

"Six hours," he replied.

Fuck. We had already been travelling for four hours. The journey from Bucharest to Galati was suddenly doubled, and little did we know that the six hours was a white lie to persuade us to go; the real figure was eight.

Three hours into the road trip, the snow was hammering down harder and harder. I saw a car skidding off the road into someone's garden, narrowly missing a group of stray dogs. Our driver was unfazed and kept going. I was in the front seat, watching the road, holding tightly onto my seat. The promoter was constantly calling us, asking for our ETA; it seemed to be getting later and later. He told us that the club was already busy — hard to believe from what we could see unless Galati had a microclimate.

The roads were getting smaller and slower; we could only see ten metres in front of us. It was a full-on blizzard. The trucks in front of us were not able to get through the snow any more, and eventually, we just stopped. There was a dead silence. I looked at the driver and said, "What happens now?"

He replied, "It looks like we are stuck here for the night."

The forecast was bleak. The snow would continue throughout the night. The driver called the promoter and told him that we were not going to make it. The roads around us were all blocked; the snowstorm was getting worse. There was no chance of any rescue. This was where we would be sleeping. I couldn't see anything out of the windows except the truck's rear lights in front of me. It turns out that we were only one hour away from the club but in the middle of nowhere. Not even a shop for at least sixty kilometres. The temperature gauge read minus thirteen degrees Celsius. We kept the engine running to heat the car. We had no food, no drinks, only the empty McDonald's cups. We started to get thirsty. I remembered watching survival documentaries that showed hikers heating snow to drink it. I took the two cups and opened the door, but the blizzard was so strong it slammed it back shut. I tried again. This time, I managed to get out. I was being knocked off my feet, such was the power of the storm. I felt like Bear Grylls, filling the cups with snow, which changed from white to a slightly brown mix of Coke Zero. I got back in the car covered in snow and placed the cups on the heater, and we took turns to drink them. This was real survival. The road was desolate, lined with trucks, the drivers all in their cabs, lights off and not a soul in sight. It was three a.m., and eventually, we fell asleep.

I woke up at six a.m. The snow had stopped, it was starting to get light, and the sky was clear. We were in a Romanian forest; everything was calm, and it was quite enchanting. It was hard to believe that just three hours earlier, we had been in a full-on snowstorm. My mouth was dry, but there was no water left. I couldn't see anything out of my window, the snow had cocooned us, and I couldn't get out. I sat there wondering what to do. We had a flight to Munich at midday. Word had got out that we were stuck in the snow, and the online brigade were fishing for info. The driver eventually woke, and we managed to open his door, the rest of the car still totally submerged. I trudged up and down, wondering what to do next. We decided to try to drive back to Bucharest to make our flight, but how would we get the car out of the snow? We didn't even have gloves to try with our hands. I went to the truck behind and knocked on the door. Someone inside stirred and opened the window. Our driver asked in Romanian for a shovel, but the guy was from Ukraine and didn't understand a word. We pointed to our car in front, and he realised what we were asking for and passed one out of his cabin. Maybe these guys were used to being snowed in.

We dug ourselves out of the huge snow mound and gave the shovel back to the truck driver. Our driver did a U-turn, and we were on our way back to Bucharest.

This time we could see how beautiful the road was. It was a postcard of white against blue; I even saw a deer run across us to complete the picture. Five hours later, we arrived at Bucharest Airport, thanked our heroic driver, and we were onto the next gig in Germany.

In this job, you have to be a road warrior; nothing was going to stop us except the gods. A soon as we arrived in Munich, Romania was history. The Romanians knew that we had done everything we could to make the gig in Galati. We went back a few months later (this time without snow) and were given a hero's welcome. Everyone knew the story. The crowd appreciated us even more that time, but we learnt new lessons. Always check the weather forecast before starting a journey in winter, and never take the promoter's word.

Romania is one of the best party countries in Europe, no doubt. Festivals like Untold and Sunwaves are two of the best in the world. The beach in Mamaia where Sunwaves is held has even been renamed "Crazy Beach", which is a perfect name, as the festival goes on for five days without stopping. It's one of the hidden gems in Europe. Whereas the less knowledgeable clubbers will go to Ibiza and Berlin, I often see the cooler kids at Mamaia.

A New Drug Experience in Escobar's Town

A call came through that I was going to Colombia. I had been waiting for this one for so long. Many of my friends in London are Colombian, and we have a great connection. They love music and going out; they have a zest for life which reminds me of Mexicans. I feel more at home with them than I do with British people, and they assured me that I would love their homeland.

The first stop was Cali. I had high hopes but was disappointed. The place was boring, unsafe, and there was nothing to see. The gig was bad, and the food was disappointing. What an anti-climax.

Bogota was the next stop, much of the same. A huge sprawling city, every day cloudy and miserable (high altitude on the equator). The gigs here are mostly good, as you would expect for the capital, and the restaurants much better than Cali, although we always go to Peruvian restaurants: Rafael and Criterion. Colombian food isn't all that. I wondered what I was missing in Colombia. After two gigs, I'd seen nothing special.

The third stop was Medellin. This was where the magic started. I expected it to be dangerous, drug gangs roaming the streets, but instead, it was a very vibrant, friendly city, picturesque, and sunk deep into the surrounding mountains. Young, big-assed brunettes walked through the streets in their own Silicon Valley. Cosmetic surgery is famously cheap and accessible here. We drove past Hooters on the way to the hotel; I didn't even know it was still going. They wouldn't have problems finding the staff here.

Every street had shuttered buildings in a rainbow of colours, shabbily stacked on top of each other. I wasn't sure if they were houses or slums, but they had a charm that I had seen nowhere else before. Taxi drivers were congregating on street corners amidst a backdrop of colourful street art and graffiti; their yellow cabs looked like they hadn't been driven for days.

The local Colombian promoter, Johnny, picked us up from The Charlee Hotel — an aptly-named, uniquely designed hotel, bang in the centre of the action. This hotel was set up for young party people: rooms equipped with DJ set-ups, Jacuzzis, well-stocked minibars, and a vibrant rooftop terrace. This was nothing like the stale, old-fashioned vibe of Cali and Bogota. Here, it felt more like Miami or Barcelona. Except the cocaine was five dollars a gram.

I had to mention the white stuff at some point. It's what everyone associates with Colombia. As my Colombian friend in London once said, if he had a dollar for everyone who asked if he sold cocaine, he would be richer than Pablo Escobar. Talking of Don Pablo, it was a subject that was off limits in Medellin. Any mention of him, his cartel, or cocaine, for that matter, was met with strong disapproval, even by the young party people. The city had been run by the Medellin Cartel for decades, until the nineties, but the legacy lives on; nobody there wants to talk about it.

Johnny was an interesting character. Born in Medellin, but randomly he went to university in Wigan in the north of England. I've never even been to Wigan myself. Someone once told me to put my foot down if I ever drive through there. I had an instant connection with him. It takes a certain kind of character to be thrown into a remote town with a new language and culture, which I could totally relate to. Johnny explained the story of Medellin and why people don't like to talk about the dark past. Escobar destroyed the city, created the narco-state, and terrorised the people. It had been liberated from the cartel rule in recent times, and the people were enjoying their peace.

I was interested in what the people at the party were into. Surely at an electronic music party in Medellin, people took something. We arrived at the party at one thirty a.m. Latinos go out late. The party was only just warming up. It was in the grounds of a beautiful villa on the outskirts of the city. It was raining, and the whole thing was outdoors, but it didn't stop the people. They continued dancing throughout the night. I could sense that something was in the air, but I had no idea what it was. I asked Johnny what they were taking, and he smiled. Tucibi. Somehow, this party gadget had bypassed me. Officially called 2C-B, it's often marketed as pink cocaine and had become the drug of choice for the Colombian elite. Made popular by models, actresses and even politicians, it had exploded in popularity in Colombia and was being pushed around the country by the cartels, while the best of their most famous export was sent to the USA and Europe.

Our artist liaison asked me if I wanted to try it. When in Medellin, I guess. He took me to the bathroom and out came the pink powder. I didn't even know if I had to swallow it or snort it. He told me to take it like MDMA. I took a small amount with my finger and washed it down with my beer. It was such a small dose that I didn't think it would affect me at all. I went back to the party. I didn't feel anything. What was all the fuss about?

About two hours passed, and I had to check myself. For the last thirty minutes, I had been completely tripping out, without even realising. The feeling crept up on me without me even knowing. For the past half hour, I had been totally zoning out before realising that I was completely wired. I was having slight hallucinations, but I always knew what I was doing. It was similar to MDMA, but it came on so light that I didn't even realise it was happening. The other DJs took it too, as did everyone at the party. Night became morning, and we were all flying; the crowd were going nowhere either, everyone on the same wave.

Everything was going wrong, but the tucibi made everything OK. The promoter's wife tipped her drink over the DJ's laptop, and the music stopped for ten minutes, but in our minds, everything was OK. We fixed it and started again. Nobody cared. The rain kept coming down hard. Usually, we would be running for cover, but the rain felt so good. Johnny reminded me that it was nine a.m. Where did the time go? We had a flight at midday to London via Bogota and Madrid, so we should go. We contemplated missing the flight. We were having so much fun, but the cost would have been insane, so we left for the airport. Our planned afterparty at the Charlee was abandoned; the jacuzzi could wait for another day. As we walked out with our drenched bags, the people continued partying; some smiled at me as we walked out. They wouldn't want to change places with us right now.

Medellin Airport is not the place you want to be high as a kite. It's a tiny, crowded, disorganised place. Eighteen-hour flights back to Europe from South America tours are always rough. The long-haul to Madrid is the easy leg. Feet up and relax. The final leg from Madrid onwards is always the killer. Monday morning in a packed Barajas Airport lounge is always hectic, crawling with perfectly suited businessmen staring at us like we shouldn't be there. A final few, glasses of Rioja before the punishing final stretch. This time the journey was tougher than usual. I stopped hallucinating somewhere over the Atlantic, staring at the flight path for the rest of the journey, paranoid that the captain would fall asleep and miss the stop.

Russia, Rabbits and Siberian Girls

I love weird countries — the weirder, the more fascinating. Russia is, without doubt, the most strange, subliminal country I have ever seen, with its Slavic neighbour Ukraine not far behind.

I've been to Russia at least fifty times. It's one of those countries where the more you go, the more interesting it gets. The cultures, values and traditions are hugely different from ours in the West, but through music, I have met some amazing like-minded people and had some of the wildest times.

I've travelled all around the country from Moscow to Siberia. It's the biggest country in the world with eleven different time zones, half of the country is in Asia and half in Europe, yet the differences from one side to the other are not so distinct. In the UK, you can drive for thirty minutes, and the accent can be massively different. In Russia, you can fly ten hours from St Petersburg to Vladivostok, and the accent is almost the same. In many towns, it's like going back fifty years in time. When the women leave the house, they don't wear anything but a dress, and high heels (even to the local store), towering over their men, whose height is irrelevant so long as they are able to pay the bills.

I first went to Moscow in 2010. I was expecting a city full of secret agents, vodka, beautiful women and flashy cars. I was partly right, but there was so much more. I had a gig at Vanilla Ninja, one of the top clubs in the city at the time. The promoter took me for dinner with six others — all beautiful women. "Welcome to Moscow; we have the womans," he said, smiling, with a cigar in his hand and a pistol on his belt. At the gig later that night, he had fully naked go-go dancers on podiums dancing to underground music with a hipster crowd. Amazing.

Everything you hear about the beauty of women in Russia is totally true. It's unmatched anywhere else in the world, but what I also noticed is just how many more of them there are than men. If you are a single man in Russia, you would have quite a selection to choose from. Most clubs operate strict 'face control' — it's very difficult to get in. They have the luxury of this option. I've seen beautiful girls, flawlessly dressed up, turned away from clubs who would have been welcomed into any other club in the world. Never any reason given. They just accept the rejection and walk away. I never understood this, but it ensures that there is the pick of the crowd in the club every night. There are always many more women in clubs than men, sometimes ten to one. This creates an amazing vibe, the opposite of many countries, where men outnumber women, which often means an aggressive atmosphere and, in many cases, fights. I never saw a fight in Russia. You just don't know who you are messing with.

The busy Moscow roads are gridlocked with traffic. The worst traffic I have ever seen, just ahead of São Paulo. Thousands of G-wagons and Porsche Cayennes cram the streets, aggressive drivers making highly dangerous manoeuvres to attempt to cut five seconds off their travel time. I saw so many accidents. Many Russians told me the system of getting a driver's licence: pay the examiner $500, and you won't need to pass the test. This, however, leads to a lot of dangerous drivers, but it's a system that suits the corrupt police, who are happy to take their kickbacks from the drivers who want to avoid jail.

Corruption is rife, but it's a system that is accepted. If you have money, you can get anything done quickly. If you haven't, you'll be at the back of the line. It's a tough place to live if you don't know the right people. Russian men live, on average, only sixty-five years (one of the lowest life expectancies in the world), compare that to British men who live, on average, seventy-nine years. Put that down to a lot of drinking hard spirits and smoking. The healthier Russian women, on average, live seventy-five years. This explains why I see so many lonely babushkas walking in the streets.

One time I was touring with a very high-profile DJ in Russia. St Petersburg and Moscow on the same weekend, flying back to London on 24 December just in time for Christmas. On arrival, the scary, stony-faced immigration officer noticed that my DJ's visa was only valid for one night. The promoter had made a mistake with the invitation, something that could easily be rectified in many countries, but the Russian system doesn't allow for errors. Neither was Moscow a place where you want to spend Christmas, especially as it's not Christmas at all. Orthodox Russians celebrate Christmas in January. We did the first gig on the Friday in St Petersburg, and the promoter spent the whole weekend trying to figure out how to extend the trip. An old Russian army officer, Denis, was one of the most connected people I knew in Moscow. If he couldn't fix this, I don't think anyone could. His assistant had given me €5,000 in cash at St Petersburg Airport to cover our flights and visa costs. I had it with me on the Sapsan bullet train to Moscow the next day. Denis met us at Leningradsky station, drove us to the hotel, and asked for the money back. "Ross," he said, "we need to do this the Russian way." He drove to the airport with the cash, my DJ's passport and ticket, and tried to explain the honest mistake that had been made. He was back a few hours later with no cash left but a promise that my DJ would be able to fly out next morning.

He had asked the Aeroflot woman to write a letter stating that the flight had been cancelled, and the passenger needed to fly the next day, and therefore needed an overstay on his visa of twenty-four hours. She refused until cash was mentioned, then she demanded €2,000 for a letter which took her three minutes to type.

Then the airport security asked for the remaining €3,000 to ensure that he got through the airport, even with the letter — Russian corruption at its greatest. My DJ made it home for Christmas, and I stayed in Moscow with my non-restricted visa for a surreal Orthodox holiday.

Surreal is the word to describe Russia. I am so fascinated with the culture. Every gig I do, I stay extra days, sometimes even weeks. Some of the coolest people I know are from Moscow, and I know more people from there than from any other city. Yes, there are the old-school Soviet types still living as if it's Stalin times, but more and more, I see friendly, open-minded Muscovites who love music, travel and everything else that we like in the West. They are very interested in meeting foreigners, as there are not many. I've felt more welcome in Russia than in any other country. They can be cold to start with, but once they open up, they really open to you. Most are blunt, direct, and they don't do small talk or niceties, which suits me fine. There are too many fake people in the world, and here you know where you stand right from the start. You won't find any kind of hyper-sensitive climate as you do in many countries in the West, overly politically correct people are always sensitive about something and go looking for agendas. In Russia, you can relax, and nobody will judge you. They live in a world where you daren't question anything, which leads to acceptance and respect for other people's views. I've never met a nation that is so superstitious and paranoid, but this just adds to the mystery. Just don't talk about politics. You won't win a discussion.

If you had asked me before 2015 which city in the world was the best for nightlife, I would have said, undoubtedly, Moscow. There were so many good clubs and events. Arma 17, Trokya, Gipsy, Gazgolder were immense, and then my favourite: Krysha Mira or "Rooftop of the World" in English. This was the definition of surreal. The party got going at five a.m. when most of the other Moscow clubs were winding down. They had the strictest face control I have ever seen. Several times I was rejected at the door, the only place in the world it ever happened, and, still, I would try again. I saw hundreds of cool, well-dressed people turned away, with just a few allowed in. I never worked out what the criteria were. Once you were inside, it was the definition of surreal. The most beautiful people, very cool music, partying hard, dancing on tables looking over the city. The party went on until the afternoon every Saturday and Sunday. International DJs who were in town to play at other clubs regularly showed up asking to play — me included. Every time I had a weekend off touring, I would spend it in Moscow, and all roads led to Krysha. They were the glory years of Moscow nightlife. I never saw anything better than this.

In summer 2014, it all came to an end. Russia annexed Crimea, the oil price crashed, followed by the rouble. The sanctions came, and so did a big government crackdown on drugs. 'Maski Show' -

masked police were frequently storming into electronic music clubs and closing them down, suspiciously never those with government connections. Bit by bit, I saw the whole thing unravel. Every month another club closed until there were almost none left. The Moscow glory years were over for now. It was sad to see this immense city become a shadow of its former self. I have so many crazy memories of Russia in general, more than any other country.

I recall getting the metro home from a club one Monday morning. I had been out since Saturday night, played my gig, then did the usual club tour. The notorious Moscow traffic was particularly bad that day, so I took the metro. I often take the metro in Moscow. Before Uber, the Russian taxi system involved standing in the street with your arm raised, waiting for some random rusty Lada to pull over. If your negotiation broke down, there would always be another one behind, ready to pull up and clinch the deal. The train was packed with commuters like always. I was standing in the corner, wearing sunglasses, trying to understand the metro map in Russian letters. I was on the right train but in the wrong direction — a regular mistake in a city where I don't understand one letter. It was the ring line. I would eventually get home the long way around.

I looked down and saw something move, something with big ears. I knew I was still wired, but I wasn't hallucinating. It was a rabbit. Now, I was in Moscow, where weirdness is normal, but a rabbit on the metro at nine a.m. on a Monday after a weekend of partying was creepy. There was a woman sitting next to him, who I presumed was the owner, but she got off the train, and the rabbit didn't. *Maybe someone else is the owner*, I thought. After several stops, there was a complete turnover of people, and of the original passengers, only me and Rabbit remained. People started to assume it was mine. I've mentioned that Russians can be closed but present a cute rabbit to them, and you will at least get a smile. One of them said something to me. I can only presume she was saying, "What a cute rabbit you have."

My stop was coming up. I didn't know what to do. Leave him on the train or take him with me. I asked a few people if they spoke English, but nobody could. In my best sign language, I explained that I couldn't speak Russian, it wasn't my rabbit, and please could someone take him. One of the women seemed to understand and nodded. I walked out of the carriage, looking back to see if she really would take the rabbit. The train pulled away, and I never found out. I hadn't slept for two days; I had just ridden the whole way around Moscow on a train with a rabbit. It was time to go to sleep, but I always wonder what happened to the metro rabbit.

Every time I went to Russia, I had a new story when I came home. The most surreal experience was when I played in Siberia. It was December 2014. I played Moscow on the Friday and a city called Tyumen on the Saturday. I was worried about the gig in Tyumen; it was

winter and minus thirty degrees Celsius in Siberia —
temperatures that I have never experienced before.
Eventually, I agreed to it. The clincher was that the
hotel, the club, and the restaurant were all in the same
building. Once I'd got from the airport to the hotel, I
didn't have to go outside again until it was time to fly
home, so I accepted. The gig in Moscow was very cool,
like always. A secret club called Mendeleev, where you
enter through an unassuming shabby takeaway noodle
bar, through a string curtain, down some winding stairs
and into a plush cocktail bar with the next room a dance
floor surrounded by futuristic visual screens and LED
lights. So typically Moscow.

Next morning, I had an early flight to Tyumen.
Three hours later, it was like I had landed in the North
Pole. The plane windows were greyed out with fog and
snow. The passengers had somehow morphed into
Eskimos during the flight. They all disembarked, head
to toe in fur, many with *ushankas*, which I swear they
didn't have when the flight took off in comparatively
warm Moscow. The bus from the plane to the terminal
stood there, still, for a lifetime, with the doors wide
open. Who knows what they were waiting for? It was
minus thirty degrees Celsius, and I was sitting there,
shivering. I had my warmest coat on, but I was a novice
compared to these guys.

I often see flights from Thailand to Moscow,
landing in mid-winter, with shirtless drunk Russian
guys getting off the plane, holding bottles of vodka. It's

a thing that men do in Moscow to show how macho they are. *What a bunch of nutters*, I thought. I wonder if they would do the same in these brutal Siberian temperatures. I wasn't going to try myself; it felt like my bodily functions were already shutting down, and my lips had frozen together. I wish I knew the Russian for, "Please shut the bus doors before we freeze to death." I hoped that someone would say it, but everyone stood there, silent.

The bus finally moved off, and we finally entered the terminal, and like always in Russia, there were two beautiful tall girls to meet me. "Welcome to Siberia," they said. "Are you ready to freeze?"

We walked out, and I felt the Siberian blast. It was like someone was shooting an ice cannon into my face. The two girls were very friendly. They spoke perfect English, took me to my hotel and checked me in, and told me to be ready at seven p.m. *What a nice welcome*, I thought, and never saw them again. I guess the promoter had found the only two people in Tyumen who spoke English to meet me at the airport, and then I was left to fend for myself. The hotel staff spoke only Russian. I tried to order room service, which was a struggle. I ended up with borsch, as it was the only thing I understood.

I went down to the lobby at seven p.m., where the promoter was supposed to meet me, but nobody came. It was also the entrance to the club and restaurant. I sat there, people watching. This was one of those sights that you can only see in Russia. The most beautiful women I have ever seen, extremely tall, skinny, in towering killer heels and black fur coats, were coming in one by one, with hardly any men. It was as if there were a supermodel factory at the end of the street, churning out these perfect women, who kept coming and coming, literally hundreds of them. I had no idea why the ratio of females to males was so high, but I was enjoying the show. I sat there for one hour in wonder of these creatures until the promoter finally came.

"Ross, I'm so sorry," he said in broken English. "I had some business to do. Let's go into the restaurant."

I told him that I was totally fine. I was enjoying watching the people. Siberia, without doubt, has the most beautiful women in the world. Not sure what went wrong with the men, though.

The dinner was terrible. I quickly realised that the food here was not very good; this was supposed to be one of the top restaurants. When you are three thousand miles away from the nearest sea, you can't expect the sushi to be fresh. I was enjoying the sights, though. The promoter walked me up to check the DJ booth where I would be playing later, and everything looked OK. It was a typical Russian-style club, where you can stay the whole night — dinner, wine, cocktails, shisha, music and dance floor. I love places like this. You never have to move, as the venue evolves all night in different stages.

Sometimes you forget how remote you are, and inevitably people won't be into the same things. The promoter somehow thought the food was great and was asking me why I didn't finish. After a while, it was the first entertainment show. Thirty minutes before I was due to play, fifty girls came out dressed like sailors. It was a dancing show in 1940s-style to the original "Candyman". Maybe Christina Aguilera's new version hadn't reached Siberia yet. It was funny, surreal, and so Russia. How could I play my underground music after this? "It will be OK," said the promoter. "In Siberia, we like to mix everything." I knew that my set was doomed. Changing the music up like this never works, and my music was too deep to follow this. It was one of those gigs where I just put my head down and got on with it. The promoter brought the dancing girls back out to dance on the floor during my set, which helped, but it was a bizarre situation and one which would only happen in Russia.

I never went back to Tyumen, but I've done many great gigs all around Russia since then. For all its problems, it's still a fascinating place. It's weird, bizarre, mysterious, often odd, but captivating at the same time. Moscow, in particular, will always hold a special place for me. Even now, it's still a true twenty-four-hour city. You can walk into almost any bar or restaurant in Moscow at any time and find a fully working kitchen. Many of the places never close. In the summer, the terraces come out and are full, with people eating and drinking outside all day and evening. In some parts, the bars and clubs are full of cool young hipsters, not dissimilar to Berlin or London. I've been to every country in Europe, every major city. In its heyday, Moscow was number one for me, and even now would stand up to most cities in the world for nightlife.

Barefoot in Ukraine

The annexation of Crimea by Russia, unfortunately, meant the end of my favourite festival — KaZantip. I always had to choose every year — Burning Man or KaZantip. I chose KaZantip every time. It was based in a small town in Crimea on the beach and went on for fifteen days, non-stop every August. It was by far the craziest festival I have ever seen. It's held in a backward town called Popovka on the north-eastern part of the Crimean Peninsula on the Black Sea. The locals were the coldest and most unwelcoming people I have ever met. Maybe they were sick of party people descending on their town every year; they certainly didn't seem to appreciate our money. The hotels were old and run-down, the food and service were awful, hardly anything worked, it was a nightmare to get to. I should have hated it, but I loved it.

Entering KaZantip from the town was like going from the past to the future. Once you walked in, you left behind the dirty old generic streets and entered into a whole new world, a Ukrainian Disneyland. It was an entire new city built on the beach: futuristic installations, outlandish costumes, fireworks, lasers shooting into the sea, freak parades and impossibly beautiful women dancing in bikinis.

KaZantip was not just a festival, it was a movement. Everyone had to carry a yellow suitcase and a viZa around their neck. You'd see people skydiving one minute and dancing in paint the next. Yoga on the beach in the morning was right next to ravers, still dancing on the sand, on LSD. The festival went on for two to three weeks non-stop, with a New Year's Eve party on 31 July. It was bizarre, it was weird, and it was magic.

I had wanted to go for years, but it was so difficult to get to. Flights from Simferopol Airport didn't connect to anywhere outside Ukraine or Russia. From London, it was a long twelve-hour journey. Then I had a call from Dubfire. He had one space on his private jet. Count me in. I flew to Frankfurt the next day and joined the Dubjet crew. We flew on from there to Bulgaria for a gig on Sunny Beach and onto Crimea.

It was scorching hot in Crimea, temperatures nudging thirty-eight degrees Celsius. The DJs were the only people there who were not from Ukraine or Russia; such was the difficulty to get there. The headliners would play the big stages at night, then move onto the beach bars in the daytime and often play into the afternoon. Our artist liaison, who introduced herself as Anastasia 911, had been working non-stop for one week. She kept her sunglasses on the whole time to hide her tired eyes but kept going like a machine.

The sun was rising, Dubfire finished his set, 911 took us down to a circular beach bar where he would play for the morning. She showed us a small private area above the bar, which was only for us; strictly nobody else was allowed in.

The temperature was soaring. I was wearing my beloved limited-edition adidas Hi-Tops, which I took off and left there, and walked down to the sand where the party people were gathered. The vibe was unreal: beautiful people with smiley faces, no VIPs, everyone dancing, as one, bare-foot on the sand surrounding the bar. We were all given pills, which were mega strong. Many of the DJs from other stages had come to join us. One of them, Ali from Tiefschwarz, said, "Ross, your eyes are rolling. Please take my sunglasses." I did wonder why people were walking away from me.

The time was flying. Before I knew it, it was mid-afternoon. Dubfire had stopped playing; I hadn't even noticed. He found me on the beach. "Ross, it's three p.m., we need to go. The jet is waiting for us."

I went back to the private area to grab my shoes, which had gone. This wouldn't usually be a big deal, but not only were they extremely rare, but I had no other shoes with me. Travelling light is the norm on tour, a spare pair of shoes a luxury. I walked to the minivan on the scorching hot floor, hopping on my heels like a dancing bear, my feet red on the top and black on the soles. The other guys were laughing; all of us completely wired. I thought maybe one of them had taken them as a joke, but unfortunately not.

No problem, I'll buy some shoes at the airport, I thought. We were flying to Bodrum in Turkey, where Dubfire was playing that night, but I would connect to a flight to London Gatwick for a connection to Lisbon, where I was playing the next day. We arrived at the airport, which was when I remembered that private jets don't fly from the main terminal. The van drove us to a small private one where our plane waited. Definitely no shops here. The captain gave me a salute and looked down at my feet.

"Where are your shoes, sir?" he asked.

"Stolen at KaZantip," I replied.

I was still not panicking. I was sure there would be a store at the next stop. I hopped along the tarmac onto the jet, trying not to spoil the beige leather seats with my dirty black feet. I remembered that Bodrum had a nice new airport with plenty of shops, so I would buy some there. Everyone passed out on the flight, except me, like always. I sat there gazing out of the window on the four-hour flight. We landed in Bodrum. I got out of the plane. The ground was still hot, even in the early evening. I recognised the Turkish promoter from a previous gig in Istanbul. "Ross, what a surprise! How are you, and where are your shoes?" The guys burst out laughing; I told him the story. He said, "Don't worry, you can buy them in the terminal, plenty of shops there." They dropped me off at the airport, and I said goodbye to the guys. I walked into the airport, my feet leaving a black trail wherever I walked.

The airport was exactly as I remembered: brand new and shiny, except all I saw were shutters closing. My flight was the last one out, and they were winding down for the evening. I walked along the concourse, looking inside every one. Two of them, sold shoes, but the shutters were down. I begged them to open back up again, showing them my black feet, but I received a blank stare. Fuck. How difficult is it to buy shoes?

I was the last to board my flight, which was full. I had the front row aisle, not one that I would normally choose, but it was the best available. The flight attendants sat opposite me during take-off, smiling. "Where are your shoes?" They giggled. I gave the same reply. I was still pretty wired, not really thinking that two EasyJet cabin crew from Bodrum to London wouldn't have a clue what KaZantip was. We took off for the four-hour flight to Gatwick. Suddenly, the temperature in the cabin became very cold. My feet felt frozen, so numb that I couldn't even feel them. My socks had been in my shoes when they were stolen. I took my laptop, which was in a zip case, from the overhead locker. I took it out, placed my feet into the case and zipped it up as tight as I could. It looked ridiculous, but it was the only thing I had to keep my feet warm. Before long, passengers were lining up for the toilet; every single one of them looked at my feet in this laptop case and sniggered at me. Some of them asked what happened. "Stolen at KaZantip,"

I couldn't wait to land and buy some shoes. Gatwick is a huge airport, so it has many shops, but we landed, and they were all shut. I didn't plan on going home as I had an early flight to Lisbon the next day. I was going to stay in the airport hotel, but without any shoes, and my feet now battered and blistered, I had to get home. The taxi driver asked me why I had no shoes. It was getting annoying now. He dropped me outside my flat, and I walked the final few metres; at least the ground was cool now.

Three flights and three countries later, I finally got home. I hopped straight in the shower and scrubbed my feet for ages until, finally, they were clean. The layers of dirt permanently stained the bath. I grabbed some new shoes (and socks), bandaged up my destroyed feet, went to sleep for three hours and was back at the airport for six thirty, ready to start a new tour of Portugal and other countries which I can't even remember.

Paris Syndrome

Paris is a strange one for me. It's the easiest capital city to get to from London, just over two hours by train, but the last one I think of going to. I've done some very good gigs there, and it's a beautiful city, for sure, but the rudeness of the people I just can't handle.

OK, I don't speak French, but I am forever apologising for it when I am there. It's the only city in the world where people can speak English, but they won't. For some reason, they don't like the Brits. I have no idea why. We don't mind them. A little bit of friendly rivalry doesn't hurt anyone, but sometimes it feels like pure hatred.

I've lost count of the times I have ordered in a restaurant, and the guy replies in French, knowing that I don't have a clue what he is saying. Then he will slam the plates down on the table in a way that only a Parisian can.

The promoter took me out for dinner before one gig. I love my Italian red wine. I saw the Barolo on the menu and ordered it. The guy looked at me as if I had pissed on the Tricolore. He did manage to find some English. "You are here in France, not Italy. Why don't you order our wine?" Pardon, maybe don't put it on the menu if you are going to get offended when people order it. The promoter intervened, and we settled on a bottle of Merlot.

It's no wonder the Japanese get "Paris Syndrome" — the psychological damage they experience when they go to Paris and expect it to be a beautiful fairy tale romantic city and leave mentally damaged. I was the same. I had to get used to it.

I remember one day waiting in the hotel lobby for the driver to pick me up the morning after a gig. He didn't show up, so I had to get a cab. I was now late and was almost going to miss the flight. I saw a taxi on the opposite side of the street and waved to him. He told me to wait, and he would do a U-turn and come around to my side. I stood there waiting. There was a guy down the street from me, with a suit and briefcase. He blatantly saw that the taxi was coming for me. He went out into the road and jumped in it before it had a chance to turn around and pick me up. For some reason, the driver let him get in. He then did a U-turn and drove right past me, the man in the back giving me a smarmy look. He was so proud that he'd got one over on me — typical arrogant Parisian.

The DJs are always cool. I think they learn early that you can't act like that and be accepted around the world. Everyone I know is decent, both in the underground and commercial scene.

I had a gig in Paris, and I flew in one night early for my friend's birthday. She was a dancer; her boyfriend

115

was a club promoter, and she had a table at his party with her dancer friends. She asked me to join. I showed up, and I was the only guy. At the table were her eight girlfriends and me. Lucky me. The club started filling up, and the tables around us got very busy. I was getting a lot of stares from guys around; they were clearly jealous of me at this table with the girls. I was getting some evil eyes. No idea why; I wasn't with any of them.

The club wasn't my vibe at all: terrible music, awful sound system. It was a pick-up club. The type of club that I hate, but I stayed a few hours to be polite.

I was standing at the table having a drink and started getting cramps in my stomach. They got worse and worse. I was talking to my friend, holding onto my stomach. I left for the bathroom. I got into the cubicle, and I collapsed on the floor. I was still conscious, but I couldn't get up. It was like someone was driving a knife into my stomach.

I must have been there for almost one hour. My friend texted me, asking where I was. I told her that I felt sick. She sent a message back, laughing, saying that I must be drunk. There were loud knocks on the toilet door, someone shouting in French. I hauled myself up and opened the door. The security looked at me and escorted me out. I stumbled across the street and slumped on the floor, not one person coming to help. One guy even walked over me.

I don't know how long I was there, but I managed to get myself up again. My hotel was only five minutes' walk away. I remember staggering down the Champs-Élysées, falling over numerous times. There was no way that I was drunk; I never get drunk like that. Someone had put something in my drink to get rid of me, for sure, one of those jealous guys.

I remember getting back to my hotel, but after that, I blacked out. I woke up in the morning on my bathroom floor, feeling like shit. I had about ten missed calls from my friend in the club, asking where I was. I replied to her, telling her that I believed I had been spiked. She told me that it's a big problem in Paris — guys spiking girls to take them home and spiking guys to get rid of them. She said that as soon as I left, some sleazy guys moved in on the table to speak to the girls, and they couldn't get rid of them.

I can't imagine if I was a girl what might have happened to me. Even as a guy, I was lucky to get home safely. This is a big problem in nightlife that needs to be addressed. I asked the club to look at the cameras, but they never got back to me.

I felt awful the next day, but I managed to do the gig. After that, I never spent more time in Paris than I needed to. In and out every time. Such a beautiful city but with big social problems.

Tear-gassed in Turkey

Turkey has some great clubs and festivals. The food is fantastic. Istanbul is one of the world's great cities, and, for me, the new airport has surpassed Singapore Changi as the best in the world.

Tours in Turkey haven't always been smooth, however. We once did a club gig in Istanbul in May 2013. It was the time when there were protests about the Taksim Gezi Park being developed. The promoter told us that it was safe to come and that the protests would be peaceful and were away from the hotel and club.

We arrived at the hotel; everything was normal. It was a hot sunny evening outside and peaceful in the streets. The promoter took us for dinner in his own restaurant, delicious Turkish food like always in Istanbul, and we were calmly sitting on the terrace. The vibe was perfect, but suddenly, everything changed.

In the distance, I could hear aggressive chants, shouting, and people running. The sound was getting closer and closer. The protest sounded like it had become violent. Suddenly, hundreds of people ran around the corner holding their faces, a trail of smoke behind them. They were running from police who were firing teargas. Some of them tried to hide in the restaurant. Everyone from the restaurant ran inside, and the staff closed the glass doors, everyone sneezing, coughing, and struggling to breathe. The peppery smell of the gas was awful; I was sneezing uncontrollably. I looked out of the window and down the narrow alley. I saw a water cannon tank pull up. The gun on the top swerved around, pointed right at us, and suddenly unleashed a powerful jet of water at the restaurant, where many protestors were still outside, trying to get their sight back. The restaurant glass shattered. At that point, the promoter told us to follow him quickly. A huge security guard led us down to the basement, through the kitchens where the chefs were taking cover. We continued to walk through basements between buildings and suddenly came out onto the street a few blocks away. The guard escorted us back to the hotel and told us to wait in our rooms. I sat watching the riots out of my eighteenth-floor window. These people were angry, and the police were taking a hard-line against them. I didn't expect or want the gig to go ahead, not after this. Twenty-two people were dead, and hundreds hospitalised. Parties were not important. The promoter called me after a few hours and confirmed that the club would not open and to stay in the hotel until I was picked up.

The next morning, everything was peaceful. There were no signs of the furore of the previous evening. The streets had been cleaned, and the buildings were already fixed. Istanbul was back to its most charming, but I had a sombre mood going to the airport once I knew about the fatalities. I had flown to Istanbul, had teargas and a water cannon fired at me, no gig, and I was now going home. A very strange day.

I've been back to Istanbul many times since, and all has been smooth, but I will never forget that incident. It reminded me that life can suddenly change in an instant. However, I had no idea that this was exactly what was going to happen to me next…

Scams and Jail

In 2013 I was at my peak. My music was doing well; a few of my tracks were high in the charts, I was playing many weekends, and on those I had free, I worked with the DJs I was managing. I had gone from earning a measly €135 per week in Ibiza to making more money than I needed. I started to look at my life and how I could improve it. I was still living in a shabby area of London. I always had a dream to move to a nice area, even just for one year.

I looked at some apartments in Central London and saw one that was perfect for me. It was right next to Paddington station, where the express train went to Heathrow Airport in fifteen minutes. Ideal for touring. I called the agency and set up a viewing. One guy showed it to me that afternoon. It was perfect, and I made an offer, which included a holding deposit, which is normal in London. The agency took the £1,500 and told me that they would get back to me once they had presented my offer to the landlord. After five days, I had heard nothing.

I sent them some emails but got no answer. Eventually, I received an email from the agency saying that I had pulled out of the deal, the apartment had gone, and therefore my deposit wouldn't be refunded. I couldn't understand it. Why were they falsely accusing me of pulling out? I really did want the apartment; I had made that clear. I had a feeling that I had been scammed.

I found the agency's office address and drove there. It was way far out east in London, nowhere near the apartment, which raised more suspicions. I pulled up and turned on the audio recorder on my phone. If this was a scam, I was going to record the whole thing as evidence. I walked into the office, and there was the guy who had shown me the apartment. He was acting in a very shady manner, nothing like the guy who I had met just a few days before.

He continued to insist that I had backed out of the deal and was refusing to give me back my deposit. His boss walked in, a large angry-looking man, who joined in the discussion, which got more and more heated. The argument went on for over an hour. I refused to leave the office until he gave me my money. I was brought up to stand up for myself and stick to my morals. I was not going anywhere. I was checking my phone for the agency reviews. Every single person had been robbed of their deposits. In many cases, the properties didn't even exist. People from overseas had paid deposits, only to be told that they had dropped out of the deal and they never saw the money again. I realised that I was just one of many who had been scammed, but possibly the only one brave enough to confront them.

He was getting aggressive, taunting me from behind his desk. "I have your money; I'm going to spend it this weekend," he said.

I replied, "On what? Six Big Macs?" — referring to his weight. This absolutely riled him; he started getting more aggressive. The insults continued to be exchanged. I was aware that I was recording the whole thing, so I was careful what I said. I made another comment about his size, and he completely lost it. He came around his desk and launched himself at me, punching me in the face several times. I fell back onto the desk behind me; my back felt like it cracked in half. I got myself back up, and suddenly, in the middle of an estate agent's office on a busy London high street, I was in a full-on fight with the owner of the company. The two other members of staff ran to the front door of the office and stood there watching. Within seconds, every one of the six desks was overturned, computers all over the floor and me and this conman were there going at it, full-on fist fighting. It was like something out of a Wild West movie.

I had blood all over my face from where he had initially punched me — it was running into my eyes — I could hardly see. My senses were fading; he got me into a headlock, still punching me in the face, which was now completely red with blood, and the punches kept coming. He was strangling me, and I was gasping for air. His two colleagues continued to watch and did nothing.

I don't look so strong, but I have worked out in the gym for almost twenty years, often lifting my own body weight. This guy was at least 120 kilos; he still had me in the headlock. While my air was getting less and less, the only way that I could think of getting out of it was by overturning him, wrestling style, which I have never even tried before.

I let him continue punching me, but I was saving my energy. As soon as I felt the moment, I used all of my remaining energy, pushed from the legs, and somehow overthrew him. I have no idea how I flipped a man so big; he went right over the top of me and crashed to the floor. It was a combination of adrenalin, survival prowess and my own strength. I saw his face on the ground, and I took my moment. I kicked him repeatedly before he had a chance to get up and attack me again. "Leave me alone, leave me alone!" he pleaded. I stopped and walked away towards the office door.

As I walked away, he got up, saying, "C'mon then, you fucker, I will kill you!"

What a coward. I thought about going back to him, but I just walked out and left it there. If I had gone back, I would have killed him; such was the adrenalin in my body.

I walked past the two shocked employees and out onto the street, my face full of blood. I went to a store to buy water; the guy behind the counter told me to stay at arm's-length. I walked to an abandoned car park, sat down against a wall, and pulled out my phone. I took a photo of my face, which was covered in blood. I washed it with half of the water and drank the rest. My mouth was so dry; the adrenalin was still running through my body.

I needed to get to a police station urgently and report it. I had the audio recording on my phone that I could give to the police, which would surely prove what happened. I quickly checked that it had worked. It was one hour and twenty minutes long. That was a long stand-off. I listened to the first few minutes, and it sounded clear — what a relief. I looked down the street and saw a police van, blue lights flashing. Imagining the lies that those conmen were telling the cops right now, it was not an option to stop. I put my foot down and headed for the cop shop.

I imagined going in and having officers take my account and listening to my recording, but there was no sign of any police. A receptionist took a brief statement and said that a police officer would contact me in the next three days. She gave me a wet towel for my face, which was still bleeding. I went home for the night, but I could hardly sleep. My back was in agony, my face full of wounds. I couldn't find one position in which to sleep. I was off on tour the next morning to Italy. The show must go on.

I landed in Rome, the local promoter and old friend, Massi, met me at arrivals. "Have you been in a fight?" he said. I told him the story, and he took me immediately to a hospital where we waited for six hours.

It was almost midnight; the gig was in one hour, so we left without seeing anyone.

I somehow got through the Rome gig, then next day, we drove to Rimini. They were two strong gigs like always in Italy, but I was just going through the motions. The amazing food that I always look forward to, I couldn't taste this time. I was permanently stressed. I could hardly stand up straight with the pain in my back; standing for hours at the gigs was tough. Any chance I had, I would lie down. For once, I couldn't wait to get back home.

Next morning, like most Sundays, I flew back to London Heathrow on British Airways. We landed as normal, but just before the gate, the captain made a special announcement. He asked everyone to remain in their seats, as there was an *issue* on board. I looked out of the window and saw a police car pull up. Two officers got out, boarded, and came directly to my seat. "Mr Evans, please come with us."

The old lady next to me, who I had chatted to all the way from Rimini to London, was looking at me in shock, as was the flight attendant. I was a BA gold member. Surely the only one ever to be arrested in handcuffs off a flight.

I was taken into the police car. The screen on the dashboard said: "Ross Evans. Wanted. Serious assault and grievous bodily harm."

I told them that I had already reported the crime a few days before, as I was the one who had been assaulted. The officers told me that the guy had dialled 999; hence it was being treated as a priority case. My report at the station hadn't even been picked up yet; they had no record of it. "We will take you to the station, and you can sort it out there," the cop said.

They took everything away from me, even the laces from my shoes. "The detective will be here soon. You can tell your story to him," said the chief, and he locked me in a cell. Two days later, I was still there.

The cell was two metres by three and had nothing but a hard bed and a toilet — not even a sink. All I did was pace up and down, four steps each way, then start again. The small hatch on my door would slam open and shut every hour, the suicide watch checking I was still alive. I could hear guys shouting in their cells all night. As night fell, the temperature dropped. I had only a T-shirt and was shivering on top of my hard plastic mattress. I asked for a blanket which they declined. I had no idea of the time, but there was a small window at the end, and I saw it was getting dark, then light, then dark again. How did I end up in this situation? I had done nothing wrong. Surely there had been a mistake. The other guy should be banged up, not me. Maybe there were cameras that recorded the whole thing, but I guess scammers don't have office cameras.

Twenty-four hours is the maximum that police can detain someone in the UK, but they applied for an extension and got it. It all seemed a bit extreme. Two days in a cell after being assaulted, it didn't seem right.

Finally, there was a knock on the cell door. "Come with me," said the officer. I was handcuffed again, bundled into a van, and transferred one hour across London. I felt like a convict. We arrived at Bethnal Green Police Station, and I was put into another cell, worse than the previous one. I paced up and down for a few hours, then finally, the detective arrived. I requested my right to a lawyer, who arrived within thirty minutes. Lawyers clearly move faster than the police. I told him the story. He could see that I was clearly stressed and sleep-deprived and told me not to answer any questions. "They will tie you in knots," he warned. "Just say, 'no comment' to everything."

I was taken to the questioning room; cameras faced me from all sides. The detective started the recorder and read out the accusations against me. If there were an award for the best fictional novel, the conman would have won it hands-down.

"Evans stormed into the office smashing up everything in his path, demanding his money back, abused me and my staff before viciously attacking me."

It was difficult to sit there and say nothing while a huge pack of lies was being read out against me.

Now was the best part. The guy reported that his £7,000 Cartier watch had gone missing in the fracas and that I was the thief. At that point, I looked open-mouthed at my lawyer, who ordered the interview to be stopped. I needed a few minutes to calm down. I had never heard anything so outrageous before. The police left the room.

"Do you know anything about this watch?" my lawyer said.

"Of course not."

It was a clear attempt at an insurance scam. The scope of the conman's lies had no boundaries. He had clearly been conning people for so long and never been caught. He thought he was invincible, but now he had come up against me.

I gave the police my phone recording and was released on bail. Walking out of that cell was so liberating. I never thought London air could feel so fresh. I hadn't seen daylight for two days and hadn't slept for four. All I wanted was a shower, some food, and to lie down.

My lawyer advised that as I had no witnesses and the guy had his staff, it was difficult for me to prove anything. There were no cameras in the office, and my audio recording, despite proving the guy's story was false, didn't show who hit who first, which was the only thing the police cared about. They didn't have time to look at the bigger picture, like the fact that this guy was a proven conman. That was too advanced for them. I was told that unless I found some evidence that proved that the guy hit me first, I was looking at six months in jail.

The next weekend I was back on tour in Belgium. Nothing was going to stop me. Antwerp has an awesome music scene, and my friend Ugur puts on the most amazing events. I was able to switch off from the shit for a day and be back among honest, open-minded people again instead of criminals and police. It didn't last for long. The next day as I was flying back into Heathrow, exactly the same thing happened. The captain made the same announcement. A police car pulled up right next to the plane, the officers came on board, and I was arrested again. I recognised one of the officers from the week before.

"Do you remember me?" I asked. "This is a mistake. You arrested me exactly the same time last week."

He looked at me for a while with a dumb blank stare. Surely he hadn't arrested many people in the last week who looked like me. "Oh yeah, I remember you. You're the one who works with music, right?" he replied. "Have you assaulted anyone again this week?"

"No, of course, I haven't, and I didn't assault anyone last week either," I replied in front of all of the passengers.

He took me off the plane and sat me in the car. I saw the same wanted sign on the front screen. It was déjà vu. I asked him to call the detective, as it was clearly a mistake. I was not going back to that cell again.

He called the detective. "Sorry, I forgot to take him off the wanted system. Let him go," I heard. Nothing was surprising me any more. The officers took me through passport control, apologised, and I was on my way. The next day, I was officially charged with assault. This was the point when I realised that the police in the UK are useless. From the front-line officers to the detectives, they didn't seem to have a brain between them. It was clear that if I were going to get myself out of this mess, I would need to do my own detective work.

The next few months were a nightmare. I couldn't plan much ahead unless I could prove that I was innocent. I turned down many tours and gigs for court cases which were mostly cancelled on the day. I did a tour of the USA on one weekend, flew back to London for a court appearance (which was cancelled hours before), then flew back to the USA again to complete the tour. I was fighting to stay afloat, more determined than ever, but I could feel my career was slipping away. I was barred from East London, the capital's party zone where the incident happened, barred from contacting the scam agency, so I couldn't get my money back. The conmen were playing dirty tricks too, constantly calling the police, falsely claiming that I was contacting them. Everywhere I turned, I hit a wall.

One court appearance was on the same day as a gig in Oslo. I arrived at court with my luggage. If the judge bailed me again, I would go direct to the airport. It was touch and go whether I would make it, but I was determined. "Don't leave your luggage in the waiting room," my lawyer said. "It will get stolen; it's full of criminals in here."

I stepped up into the dock right in front of the judge with my luggage. "Why do you have your luggage?" he asked. "Are you pleading guilty and going directly to jail?"

"No, sir, I'm not guilty. I'm going on tour."

The judge laughed and bailed me to appear at a later date. I went directly to the airport and flew to Oslo for the gig. I was totally living on the edge.

A few months passed with no news, apart from a few dirty tricks and death threats by the conmen, which I was now used to. Then, I received a breakthrough. My lawyer received the case papers. One of the staff members in the office that day hadn't given a statement — the conman's own staff member, who saw everything. Something was up here. I knew the guy's first name from the recording, but that was all. I spent weeks and weeks searching social networks, sending messages to hundreds of guys in London. Finally, one of them replied. "Ross!" he said. "I've been trying to find you." It was a huge moment.

He was just a young kid. He had been trying to find me but also only knew my first name. I was not allowed to speak to him, other than confirming that he was the right person, so I passed him to my lawyer.

His story was shocking. After I had left the office, the owner got the two staff members together. He told them that the police were coming, both of them had to say that it was me who started the fight, or they would lose their jobs. One agreed, but this one refused, as it was not the truth. He was told to pack his things and leave the office immediately before the police arrived and never go back. I was heartened that someone had such strong morals; it would have been so easy for him to lie and keep his job. It felt that this was the moment that would turn things around.

My lawyer went to meet him. He gave his full version of the story and signed his statement. The letter was sent to the Crown Prosecution Service. It felt like justice was finally coming, but then came a huge setback.

The CPS replied, saying that they would not accept the letter; the witness had to appear at the trial and give his evidence. The conmen had threatened him that if he went to court and testified, they would come after him. He was too scared to go. Disaster. I couldn't believe that the UK justice system was so flawed and could be played by criminals so easily.

Fourteen months after the date of the incident, the trial date was finally set. My lawyer told me that it couldn't be delayed again; this was D-day. It was now June, festival season was in full swing, the first Sonar Festival in Barcelona I had ever missed.

My lawyer regularly contacted the witness, offering him protection. He started to come around to the idea of coming to court, but he was scared. It was still touch and go if he would show up. I watched countless documentaries on how to survive in jail, I clearly wasn't cut out for it, but I was prepared. Six months would have been three with good behaviour. Maybe it wouldn't be so bad.

It was the eve of the court date. I was polishing my shoes, still thinking that it can't be real. I spoke to my barrister, and we went through everything. We found hundreds of people who had also been scammed by the conmen. I even had the BBC Watchdog show tracking them with hidden cameras, but I still needed to prove my innocence. I had never been so nervous before. I was never good at public speaking. Give me a crowd of five thousand people at a festival to play music to, but talking to a group of people — I always went to pieces. It came down to one thing. If the witness showed up, I was free. If he didn't, I was probably going down. It was a knife edge. Then came a call that finally changed everything.

It was eleven p.m. the night before the trial, and my lawyer called me.

"Ross, can you speak? I have some good news."

The court case had been dropped. The conmen found out that the witness was coming to the trial and got cold feet. They would have been shown up in court, and their whole scam business would be blown. I felt a sense of relief that I can't even describe. Fourteen months of battling, sleepless nights, hitting so many obstacles but never giving up.

So many questions remained. Would the witness have shown up at court? Which way would the trial have gone? In some ways, it was worse that it didn't go ahead. I never got the chance to prove my innocence. I could have revealed the extent of those guys' criminal activities, but I never had my chance in court. I was just relieved that I didn't have to stand in front of those men in the dock.

My lawyer made contact with the agency to start a civil case, but they had closed down a few weeks before the trial date. Scammers don't stick around for long. The owner is now in Cape Town, posing as a Michelin star chef (with no qualifications) cooking at rich people's houses. I would love to believe in karma, but from my experience, I don't see any evidence that it exists.

I learnt a lot from that episode. Never pay deposits to someone before checking them out, don't trust the police to do their work, and always have a witness. Do I regret going to the office that day? No. I would do the same again. Next time with video. I always stand up for my values and never give up. If we don't stand up to criminals, we are giving in to them.

I was tormented and distressed, permanently scarred. To this day, every time I see a uniformed person in an airport, I think it's police coming to arrest me. I never trusted anyone the same way again. My music career was in tatters, all because of these awful people. I sued the police for wrongful arrest — twice which was a mammoth process but I won. They admitted their failings, and we settled out of court. I was done with the UK, the systems were broken, and I moved back to Barcelona for a fresh start.

Red Mist

I'm from a tough background. Newport is, without doubt, one of the roughest towns in the UK. I can't ever remember being in the school playground without seeing a fight, and that was just the girls. There was always someone 'after you' for no real reason; I was forever looking over my shoulder. Most of my friends ended up in jail before school was out. Weekends out in the town were like a battle zone.

I was looking for an escape route, which electronic music gave me. I still, however, have the hard exterior. If someone shows me aggression, I can return it back to them times ten. Sometimes this gets me into trouble.

When you are on tour, it's a high-intensity environment. Some people are out of their minds; crazy things can happen. Security can be aggressive, as can often the clubbers. Often the maddest things can happen in the unlikeliest of places.

It was my first time in Puerto Rico. It was three days of paradise, beautiful beaches, clear waters, pool parties and some of the nicest people I've ever met in the world. Next day was a nine-hour flight to San Francisco, connecting in Dallas.

We arrived at San Juan Airport. The line for security was huge, snaking right around the terminal. I was again on tour with Nic Fanciulli, who had played a mammoth-long set the night before. We stood at the end of the line. An old lady lining up behind me, who should never have been waiting at her age, picked up my accent, and we started talking. I told her to go to the front, but she was happy to wait. Everyone was waiting patiently; they were on the same flight as us. We were almost at the front when two guys dressed in suits strolled into the terminal and cut into the line right in front of me. Maybe they were going to miss their flight, but there was no apology or acknowledgement of the people behind. I hate people who push in. In the civilised world, it's not acceptable.

"What are you doing?" I said, but they completely ignored me. They emptied their pockets and put everything into trays. I was next. I placed my MacBook and electronics into my tray, which was sliding on rollers. I noticed that between the rollers and the X-ray machine, there was a big gap. I was going to teach them a lesson — never push in front of people.

I nudged my tray, which pushed the guy's tray forward, and it fell down the gap. His phone, coins, watch and other things were all over the floor. I giggled to myself. He turned around and looked at me, picked up my tray and threw it against the wall. My MacBook, my most important possession, opened up and landed in a V-shape on the deck, with everything else I owned sprawled around it. Nobody touches my MacBook and gets away with it. We were right in front of the metal detector with the security guards all around, but I saw red mist and thumped him in the face. I heard a gasp from the passengers around me. I don't know who was more stunned, the guy or me. He launched himself towards me, grabbing my neck, but I stood still, realising what I had done. This was not the place to hit someone, right in the middle of airport security, hundreds of people around. Even if he had thrown my MacBook.

Four security guards jumped in and separated us; they pinned me to the wall. "You hit him; you hit him!" they repeated. I tried to tell them that he had thrown my tray, but they were not listening. Nic was looking at me with his head in his hands. The guards were discussing what to do, it was all in Spanish, and I couldn't understand. I was still being held against the wall. Things were looking bad; I was resigned to the fact that I was not going to San Francisco. Maybe a San Juan jail cell was awaiting. All of the passengers were stood there watching. "The show's over guys, continue through the machine", one of the police bellowed.

Suddenly, everything changed. The old lady behind me called the security over. She had seen everything and told them what happened. There were a lot of discussions taking place, and I had no idea what was going on. I stood there waiting. The flight was boarding, and the two businessmen had long gone.

The head of security called me over. "We are very sorry for what happened, sir. Please can you check to see if your laptop is working? If it is broken, you can claim a replacement one from us."

I couldn't quite believe the turnaround. He watched me check my laptop. I switched it on, and it was working OK. Just a small dent, but I would live with that. The old lady behind me had saved me. I never had a chance to thank her; she was already gone. I was demoted to the back of the plane, away from the two guys and everyone else, and told not to move from my seat. But at least I was flying. It could have all been so different, but at least I taught that man a lesson not to push in.

When you work in nightlife, the fact is that you will encounter many people drunk, under the influence, and behaving uncivilised. People in clubs trying to enter the DJ booth are a constant problem. Many people feel that they have the right to be there, but they have no reason to be. Sometimes there is security keeping order, but often we have to deal with it ourselves. I always say the same thing, "Please go to the dance floor; it's the best place for you." Some people listen and realise; many continue to try to force themselves in. The more wasted they are, the worse it usually is. I've received punches and threats all over the world. I guess an average security guard receives these every night, but often the security themselves are the problem.

I am a regular at Pacha Barcelona. Sunday nights are their best night of the week; this is the night when the real clubbers in the city come out. One night, two of my DJs were playing; it was absolutely packed, the vibe was superb. Easily the best weekly Sunday night in the world.

After a few hours, I needed the bathroom, but the club had just been refurbished, and everything had changed. I went into the empty cubicles, but when I came out, two big security guards were waiting for me. I showed them my wristband. It clearly said, "Artist," which usually gains you entry into anywhere, but these two grabbed me aggressively, bundled me up the stairs and pushed me out of the door and out of the club. I tried to explain to them that I was part of the artist team, but they told me to get out. I was standing outside telling them, but nobody would listen. After a long wait outside, the promoter finally came out and got me back in. If I, the DJ's manager, was being treated like this, then imagine how the clubbers were being treated. I sent in a complaint to the club. The next day I received an email from the head of security apologising. He said that he had sanctioned the two security guards and would change the culture there. I don't know if he actually did, but it was refreshing to receive a message like that admitting that they were in the wrong. No doubt he would have watched the cameras and been shocked at how his guards treated me. Overzealous security guards are a big problem in certain countries. The best guards are the most chilled ones. It's 2021; there is no need to be acting like a tough guy in clubs.

I was at a festival in Chile, where usually the people are super nice. I went to the private artist toilet behind the stage, and suddenly a hand grabbed my arm, mid-piss, and yanked me backwards down three steps, and I landed on my back. It was the security guard. He was telling me in Spanish that I was using the wrong toilet, even though I couldn't see any signs anywhere, and the whole toilet area was empty. I got up and showed him my artist wristband, but he just started pushing me. I lost it and completely showered him with punches, left him on the floor and walked calmly back to the stage. Thirty minutes later, his boss came into the booth and told me that I had hurt one of his staff and asked me to leave the club. Luckily, my DJ had just finished, and we were leaving anyway. That could have been tricky. Chilean security guys are not to be messed with. I just couldn't understand why he was so aggressive towards me for using a toilet backstage.

It's not always guards and men who can be problematic. Often, it's the girls too. One night in Toronto, a girl in the booth was drinking all our drinks. I let her take them, as she claimed to know the DJ I was working with. She was downing the vodka and was getting more and more drunk. I was keeping an eye on her. The club staff continually came over asking if she was with us, they wanted to kick her out, but as she was the DJ's friend, they let her stay. Eventually, she fell over in the booth, almost spilling her drink over my DJ's laptop. That was the moment when I had to step in and tell her that she needed to leave the booth.

She suddenly started punching and kicking me like a complete psycho. I stood there completely still with my hands by my side and let her do it, as the whole club could see what was happening. I would never touch a female. The security came over and threw *me* out of the club. I told them that they had it totally wrong, but once again, they wouldn't listen. The promoter (who had seen the whole thing) came over and rectified the situation, and they eventually kicked her out. The security, once again, had to apologise to me. He admitted that he saw a scuffle involving a girl and instantly assumed that she was the DJ's wife, and I was a random, so he kicked me out before thinking twice. We continued the night without the psycho girl, who was waiting outside, sending us threats, before giving up and going home. We never heard from her again. These are the kind of crazy freaks who we meet on our travels.

A few months later, we were in Montevideo, Uruguay, at an amazing outdoor party. We allowed some of the cool local girls who we knew into the booth, but their male friends tried to follow them in. I said no as we didn't know them, and they were in the VIP area behind anyway. I told one of the guys that he couldn't come in, and he punched me right in the stomach and ran off. I completely saw red mist and chased him backstage, but he disappeared off into the car park, and

I lost him. I would have hit him so hard he wouldn't have walked back. Latino guys are very territorial, and I was some gringo in his country telling him where he could not stand, and he didn't take to that very well. Patrick's words of advice were ringing in my ears that night when I went home. I try to make everyone feel welcome at the events and give good vibes to everyone. But being punched for telling someone that they can't come into the DJ booth is excessive.

The same happened in Cape Town a few weeks later. It was the Ultra Music Festival after-party at one of the clubs in the city. The Ultra crew are amazing — one big family, and the after party is where everyone comes together to party after all of their hard work at the festival. The whole crew were on stage with Nic Fanciulli playing. Some of the crew noticed that a random guy had found his way into the stage and was annoying everyone. I asked him politely to leave the stage. He wasn't happy about it but he stepped down to the dancefloor. One of the Ultra crew came over to say thanks to me. Suddenly I felt this massive blow to my stomach. The guy had taken a run up and punched me hard in the gut, I was totally winded. The security guard saw it and escorted him out. I was relieved that he had been kicked out and I didn't have to look over my shoulder. Then, thirty minutes later I saw him back in the club, staring at me. I asked the security why he was back in. He told me that he was from a very rich powerful family and they had to let him back in. I had to spend the rest of the night watching him snarling at me from the dancefloor, wondering who might be waiting for me outside. Once again, I had got myself into trouble by trying to do the right thing.

Flying Club Conquered

A few DJs suggested that I get the frequent flyer cards of the main airlines, as I was starting to fly so often. I signed up for all of them, and before long, I was rising up the status levels until I reached maximum status across all of the airlines. I could access all of the best airline lounges in the world, and I was often upgraded to business or first class, which made everything much more comfortable. I realised that these flying clubs were very cliquey, with many people displaying their status on their luggage to show off. I often saw full-grown men and women taking their luggage down from the overhead compartments and making sure that they did it in a way that everyone saw their gold British Airways card. Pretty sad if you ask me. Often, they buy flights that they don't even need, just to keep their status so they can use the lounges, but the needless flights that they buy are worth more than the use of the lounges themselves (which you can pay to use anyway) and the airlines are having the last laugh. I remember being one flight short of my status with one day left until the end of their calendar year, so I bought a flight that evening just to keep the status. I was being sucked in too.

It got to a point where it was strange when I was in one of the airport hubs at the weekend, and I *didn't* see a DJ. Tiefschwarz, Tiga, Groove Armada, Danny Tenaglia, Luciano, Jamie Jones Joris Voorn — I used to see these guys like this frequently on my travels. I remember once helping Josh Wink use the printer in the business lounge in London Heathrow and helped him iron his shirt in Bergen in Norway a few months later. Artists truly are global citizens, and we cross over the world every week in any country.

I'm not your average business class traveller with the way that I dress; I never wear a shirt or suit. When I'm sitting in business, I often get some stares from the well-dressed people. One flight, however, will forever stick in my mind.

I was on a flight from Amsterdam to London one morning at eight a.m. I took my seat in business class. I was sitting next to a French guy who took a lot of offence that I was sitting next to him in the same class. He called the flight attendant and said to her in French, "Please can you check if this guy is supposed to be sitting here? I don't believe that he should be in business class."

I understood most of what he said (from my school French). I was so shocked that I didn't say anything.

Then the flight attendant came out with an iPad and asked me to confirm my name. She turned to the Frenchman and said, "Yes, this gentleman is supposed to be sitting here."

The man shrugged his shoulders in the Parisian way, muttered something and gave me a glare. He had a huge problem that I was in business class and didn't look like someone who he imagined should be sitting there. I thought about *accidentally* spilling my drink over him, but it was an early flight, and I didn't have the energy to say or do anything. When we landed at London City, I pulled down my luggage from the overhead bin and put it next to his. Both pieces of luggage had the Air France-KLM airline tags. His was gold; mine was platinum (the higher level). I made sure that he noticed it. "Look at that," I said. "Never judge a book by its cover."

He walked off the plane, mumbling. I knew that I had completely spoilt his day. The flight attendant also apologised to me when I disembarked the aircraft, as she should never have questioned me in front of him.

I became such a frequent flyer that the cabin crew used to recognise me. I started to become a flight nerd, remembering routes, staff, flight numbers; I even know that the first flight into London Heathrow at 04.50 every morning (the flight that wakes up every light sleeper in West London) is the BA32 from Hong Kong.

Soon my miles were starting to accumulate, so much so that when I had free days off, I would use the free flights to go to other countries that I hadn't visited before. While DJing and touring, you rarely get to see the places that you go to. It's often airport, hotel, club, airport. I've been to Rome about fifteen times, but I've never seen the Colosseum, which some people might find crazy, but that's the DJ life. I will see it one day.

But on my days off, I am more interested in using my miles to go to less well-known corners of the earth, such as parts of Russia, Brazil, Ukraine, Cuba, Cambodia, Belarus, Panama, South Africa, Estonia, Scandinavia — the less obvious places. I've stayed in some beautiful spa hotels in Belarus, seen Angkor Wat in Siem Reap, one of the Seven Wonders of the World. I've been wine tasting in Stellenbosch, South Africa, and on top of Table Mountain and dined at the King of Spain's favourite restaurant in Havana, which is actually someone's home. I've attended Subliminal festivals in Ukraine and Russia, where it felt like I was in a parallel universe. I've witnessed mid-summer solstice in Iceland, which was magical. These are all fascinating places in the world, very different to my own culture, and many of them I discovered when we had done a gig there, and I went back to discover more if I liked the feel of the place. I travelled to all of these countries with my mileage points which are one of the biggest perks of touring.

There are only a handful of airports in the world that I haven't seen. My favourite airports are: Singapore, Istanbul, London Heathrow Terminal 2, and Hong Kong. The famous carpet at Singapore Airport is so cosy it makes me feel like lying on it, and of course, Jewel is a tourist attraction in itself.

DJs who fly a lot usually spend as little time in the airport as possible before their flights, as they become efficient in getting through security and their gate without making a day of it like the annual holidaymaker.

For the frequent flyers, it's the lounge where we spend that last final hour before the flight. At London Heathrow, I'll always have chilli con carne and a glass of wine before getting on the flight. It's very relaxed: many businessmen working, the chairs are very comfortable and, sometimes, if my flight has been delayed or cancelled, I've gone to sleep in there for a few hours. They even have a massage centre. I often bump into other DJs I know in there, and you often see celebrities too. I once sat next to Rosie Huntington-Whiteley and Tony Hadley at the same time. People expect that if you are in the first-class lounge, you are a somebody, I guess, and open up. Rosie asked for my mixes, which I sent her for years after we met, and she always replied, saying that she used them for her exercise routines. Pretty cool.

Hong Kong Business Lounge has a chef that cooks the most amazing food to order, and it's also like a big shopping mall. You can never get bored in these airports. Four-hour stopovers fly by. The new Istanbul Airport is like Dubai Mall — I could spend a whole day there and never get bored. When I have time in an airport, usually I'm in the electrical store buying cables and gadgets that we always use when we are on tour.

I don't usually go shopping for clothes in airports, as we don't have the space to carry them around (we never check in bags as a rule). As far as food airports go, I love Rome Fiumicino — they have the best Italian restaurants, as you can imagine. Everything is super fresh. I always go to the same place and have mozzarella and octopus salad. Italians do it better.

Some of the airports in the world are not a problem to spend time in, but others, especially in remote towns or the smaller Brazilian cities, we try to spend the least time as possible as there is often nothing to do or eat, no Wi-Fi and sometimes not even anywhere to sit. Without doubt, the worst airport for me is Mykonos. It's like a squat. Considering they are trying to market the island to high-end clientele, why not start with an airport which actually has shops and places to eat... or even seats! It's a shambles.

Three's a Crowd in Barcelona

I was back living in Barcelona. One of my DJ friends came from London to visit me for a few days before Christmas. I played at Input on the Saturday night, which is one of the city's best clubs. On the Monday, we went to the Nou Camp to watch a Barcelona game. It was a standard win for Barcelona, 4–0; Messi scored, of course; they didn't even break a sweat. The game was boring, so once it had finished, we decided to go out. We went to the W Hotel where I had got a room for us for the night. The top floor bar, Eclipse, always had some kind of party going on, but as it was a weekday in December, there were not many people, so my friend and I just stood at the bar, talking.

Suddenly, we heard this really loud annoying American voice, "Hey, guys, are you from Barcelona?"

We turned around, and there was this blonde American girl. She wasn't beautiful, she seemed to be very drunk, but we were polite and spoke back to her. We told her that we were British, and she was like, "Woooo, I've met two sexy Barcelonians! Salud! Nice to meet you guys. Woooooooo!"

Firstly, I don't believe the word "Barcelonians" exists in the English (or Spanish) dictionary. Secondly, we had clearly told her that we were British, but that didn't seem to register with her. I found her too annoying, so I turned around, but my friend was speaking to her, and I overheard the conversation. She was on holiday from Florida with her boyfriend (who was back in their penthouse suite downstairs). He had taken her on a tour of Europe. So far, they had just landed in Barcelona and were on their way up to France the next day. Apparently, they had just had an argument, and she had decided to leave the room, go to the bar and get drunk.

She was so annoying, but the more drinks that I had, the more tolerant I became. We all sat at the bar doing shots for a few hours until we were all pretty drunk. As soon as she heard that I was a DJ and mentioned some of the big DJs who I managed, she was drooling. It was closing time at the bar, so we walked out, but instead of going to her room, she followed us to ours.

I came out of the bathroom, and she had already pushed the two beds together and stripped off her clothes. She stood there and said, "Come on, guys, take me. Both of you."

My friend turned off all the lights, so it was pitch black, and we basically got down to it. We couldn't see anything; it was as sloppy as hell, but this girl was absolute filth and wanted everything from us. A threesome is different from normal sex; you have to take turns, and one of the three is usually waiting around. My friend was banging her next to me, so I tried to offer something extra by putting my finger in her ass. She seemed to like it, from the noises that she was making, so I did it some more while I was waiting for my turn.

Then I heard the two of them change positions, so I pulled my hand back, waited for them to get at it again and put my hand in again. In the darkness, I found her ass again. This time she was a bit tighter, but I assumed that was because of the break and changing positions.

I tried to loosen her up, but this time it wasn't happening; she was as tight as a nun. How could she had tightened up so quickly? I ran my hand up her back to her neck but couldn't feel any hair. Then I realised my epic drunk fail — I had been fingering my friend's ass instead of hers!

I was like, "Ugh, why didn't you tell me?"

My friend was so drunk that he hadn't even realised and said that he couldn't feel anything. I got up to the bathroom to wash my hand, feeling absolutely disgusted with myself that I had been touching a guy's ass. I must have washed my hand about fifteen times, but the trauma was still there. Meanwhile, my friend was smashing the hell out of her next door. I thought, *Right, now it's my turn. I need to touch a girl again to make me feel better.* I went back into the bedroom, the light from the bathroom lit up the place, and sure enough, my friend was still banging away.

I said to him, "OK, my turn now."

"OK," he said and moved aside.

I don't think she even noticed the change; I just continued where my friend left off. Suddenly, I heard my friend spring up, and he tried to jump over us, then all I could hear were these loud vomiting sounds, and there was red liquid all over my body. I turned on the light, and he had vomited out the Catalan blood sausage that we had eaten at the Nou Camp. He'd tried to make it to the bathroom to puke it up but hadn't quite made it, and it was all over me, the girl, the bed and there was a trail to the bathroom. Everything was red. The girl and I stopped what we were doing and just heard loud vomiting noises coming from the bathroom. Total vibe killer. She said, "Is he OK?"

I went to check on him, and he'd just had to vomit it all out. We had all drunk too many shots, and the occasion had got to him. The whole hotel room stunk of vomit. The girl put her clothes on and said, "Well, thank you, guys. It was a pleasure to meet you," as if it were the most normal thing ever, and went up to her penthouse, back to her boyfriend, to continue their romantic trip around Europe.

I don't know if she and her boyfriend lasted the whole trip, but whoever he was, I felt sorry for him that he had such a filthy slut of a girlfriend. I can only imagine how much money he spent on her for that dream trip around Europe, and she was cheating on him behind his back with "Barcelonians". American girls are renowned for being slutty, but even I was shocked by that.

My friend came around, and we both sat around, laughing at the whole thing. We tried to clean up as much of the red vomit as possible and went to sleep. I woke up first in the morning and walked to the closet in the corner of the room with my open luggage and found that my clothes were covered in red vomit. It turned out that my friend had taken a wrong turn in the dark and went to the closet first to start vomiting before realising he was in the wrong place. We spent half the day trying to get my clothes and the hotel room clean.

Barcelona is definitely one of the sin-cities of Europe; the three years that I lived there were some of the wildest of my life. It's one of the three cities where most of the European music industry live (along with London and Berlin), so the other DJs and I often had big nights on weeknights, as we were away on weekends. I still rate Barcelona as one of the best places in Europe to live, especially in the summer months. It's vibrant, the food is as good as anywhere in the world, there are so many things to do, and a lot of slutty tourist girls if that's what you're into.

It's a city close to my heart, and had it not become so dangerous, I would still live there to this day. I love the architecture, the food, the weather, the artistic community, but if you don't look like a local, it is quite a dangerous place to live. I was the victim of attempted robbery at least six times in the years that I lived there, and the final straw was when three guys were trying to rip my watch off my arm in broad daylight on one of the main streets, Via Laietana, with hundreds of people around (who did nothing to help). I realised that it was not a place that I could live any more. Such a shame, as it has the potential to be the best city in the world, they just need to sort the crime out. Everyone gets robbed there; I don't know one person who hasn't.

Deep Dish Reunion

The two Deep Dish guys: Dubfire and Sharam, are two of my closest friends in dance music. I mentioned earlier in the book that I was due to go on tour with them, opening for them at every show, then they suddenly broke up as most DJ duos eventually do. They both went their separate paths, and both did very well. I even lived with Dubfire in Barcelona for one summer, which was one of my best summers ever.

Sharam is one of the most charismatic guys in the business. Dubfire is extremely kind, loves food even more than me, and is on my level in every way. They both have the same dry humour as me. I love it when people from totally different parts of the world have a connection. They both came from Iran to the USA as young kids and made their way from nothing right to the top. I have total respect for them as musicians; I love their company.

In 2015, I got the call that they were getting back together, and they wanted me to be tour manager for the whole project. Exciting times! Deep Dish were one of my inspirations when I was growing up; their music back in the nineties had a big impact on my life. When they broke up in 2008, it was a sad loss for the industry;

they made so many great tracks, and some of their sets were legendary. Would they be able to recreate that again, eight years later? They had gone in very different musical directions; Dubfire went the techno route while Sharam had created his own more commercial sound. Could they find a common sound in between to make it work? I was worried about how it would turn out.

The first gig was Chicago, home of the Deep-Dish pizza. A perfect city to start. It was an unannounced gig, listed only as "secret guests", but it was clearly the worst kept secret in town. We arrived at the venue to see the crowd lining up right around the block. It was a freezing cold mid-winter snowy night, but it didn't stop the people. Any doubts that we had were soon overcome. The atmosphere was intense; the guys played an amazing set. Deep Dish was back, and it felt great.

The tour continued: Canada, the USA, South America and into Europe. Some gigs were very good, but the musical and personality differences between the two guys became more and more apparent as the tour went on. Little problems soon became bigger ones, and the tension was mounting.

One gig in particular in Sofia, Bulgaria, was the crunch point. It was a huge events hall sell-out show; everything should have been perfect. The guys were two hours into a three-hour set. Dubfire was clearly irritated. He walked off stage, and I followed him. I asked him what was up. "This music Sharam is playing — it doesn't work with mine. I am not going back on."

I put my arm on his shoulder and tried to calm him down. I said to him, "Look, let's just get through this one. You only have one more hour. Finish the gig, and then we can work out any problems tomorrow."

He reluctantly went back onto the stage and finished the gig. Sharam could feel the tension. He knew what was up and changed the music direction for the last hour. The gig finished, the Bulgarian crowd showed their appreciation, and they clearly went away happy. But it didn't sweep the problems under the carpet.

Over the next few days, there were emergency management conference calls with all parties trying to iron out the problems in order for the tour to continue. There were some heated arguments, some home truths came out, and the tour continued, but it was clear that the chemistry was just not there. It was the wrong moment; the two guys had just grown too far apart.

We did twelve Deep Dish comeback shows. Some of them clicked, and some didn't go so well. When two DJs play back-to-back, anything can happen. Sometimes it works, sometimes not. I never understand why DJs don't talk to each other before a back-to-back set and plan things in advance, but they never do. It's often a lottery whether it works or not. But this was Deep Dish — the biggest DJ double-act in the whole world. They should have been on the money every time. Often, it felt forced and not natural. It was just not the right time for the comeback. Some of the gigs were awesome. Warung in Brazil was especially good, but many were disappointing by the guys' own high standards.

I believe that they will be back again one day, and the magic will return. There were definitely moments of it. Music goes in cycles; eventually, they will be on the same page again.

DJs and Divas

The truth is that the music industry is full of complicated, egotistical people, from the artists to managers to the club owners. The general rule is this: the more money or fame, the bigger the egos become. I've watched people become absolute monsters when the cash starts flowing in. Some keep their feet on the ground. These are the people I prefer to spend my time with, but many become twisted-up narcissists. For someone like me, it can be very difficult to watch.

I've worked with a mixed bag of people down the years; I've had to learn how to handle them. You can't always choose who you do business with. The first time I experienced fake people, it was something new to me. Why would anyone behave like that? Later I learnt that not all of us have the same upbringing with the same values. Some people don't have many morals or values; you just have to accept that and learn how to deal with it. I try to stay grounded and keep the people around me grounded too. It's so easy to change for the worst when everyone is saying yes to you. Always have someone around to call you out.

With DJs, many of them do stay on the ground, more so in the underground scene. These are the ones who I prefer to spend time with. Commercial music is a different story. The prizes are bigger; this is where the egos get huge. I've worked with a few DJs at different stages of their careers. When everything is rosy and the artist is doing well, their mood is usually good. When they are no longer flavour of the month and the gigs and fees go down, when other artists start being billed above them, this is when they start to lash out, blaming their agents, managers — everyone but themselves.

Nobody likes to go backwards in their life. DJing can be a short career; not many still perform into their fifties. You have to constantly evolve and stay relevant. If you can't find a way, your career will be a short one.

It's refreshing when you see an artist who is at the top of their game and still stays humble. Carl Cox is one. A shining example of someone who is right at the top, forever smiling, laughing, and giving out good vibes. Not a bad bone in his body and an inspiration to everyone around him. I love spending time with Carl and feeding off his energy.

American artists are often the biggest divas. This goes for all entertainment. In the USA, if you have a small amount of fame, people put you up on a pedestal. This often leads to artists becoming prima donnas. I've worked with a fair few of them.

I did a few tours, managing one American artist who was extremely temperamental. You never knew what mood he would arrive in; it depended on the day. One time we did a live show in Marseille, and he arrived in a particularly strange mood. He was a big name in France. For sure, the gig was going to be crowded, but I had a feeling that it wouldn't go well.

People in France are very vocal, and Marseille is not a city where you want to do a bad show. If they don't like something, they will let you know. He started to play, but it was not going well. An artist's mood definitely affects their performance. If you are not feeling good, you won't play well.

After one hour, a few people started booing. I was watching from the side of the stage. I'd never seen an artist get booed before. He had totally lost the crowd, and whatever he did, he couldn't get them back. He then started hiding under the booth, and the crowd couldn't see anyone on stage. The boos got louder and more vicious. The people were not dancing, just standing there shouting and showing their disapproval.

He somehow managed to get to the end of the performance. The music stopped, and a barrage of sound hit as people booed at the top of their voices. This was France, they pay their money, and they let you know when they are not satisfied. He stood there for a few minutes, booing back at them, like a football match with two opposing fans going at each other. It was one of the most surreal things that I've ever seen.

It was hostile. I was worried there was going to be a riot. Marseille is not the safest city at the best of times. I escorted him off stage and safely back to the dressing room. He asked me my opinion, and I told him honest and straight up that it was awful. I felt sorry for him in a way. The next night in Paris was much better. It's amazing what the right mood can bring to a performance.

A few weeks later, the same DJ and I were in Copenhagen. He called my room in the afternoon. "Tonight, I wanna play wearing a cape," he said. "Can you find one for me?" One of the more bizarre requests that I've ever had, especially in a city that I don't know so well. I don't like to say no, so I went cape hunting around the town. I somehow managed to find one, just a few minutes before the shops closed. He loved the cape and wore it for every show for the next few months. It made him feel like he had wings, apparently. I was happy with my can of Red Bull.

The people around you can forge your personality. Being surrounded by egoists and complicated characters isn't good for you. If you are down to earth and grounded, eventually, you could be swayed in their direction. I was sick of uncomfortably asking promoters to bring M&M's with the red ones taken out on his request; it was ridiculous. I refocused on my own music more, and for any artists who wanted to work with me, I would be careful to check out their characteristics before agreeing.

Dance like an Argentinian

Ask any underground DJ which is the best country in the world to play, and ninety per cent will say Argentina. For me, it's the ultimate place for parties. Argentinians are top of the league of global party people. The size of the crowds who show up just for one DJ is unprecedented; the events sell out faster than any other country, the people go crazy on hearing a kick drum.

They even have their own dance going on, different from any other dance I've seen anywhere in the world — they kind of roll their shoulders side to side instead of bobbing up and down. Watch any video clip of an Argentinian party, and you will see what I mean. When you are watching from the DJ booth, and you see ten thousand people all dancing that way, almost in tandem, it's a weird sight.

If you are a meat and red wine lover, it's the Holy Grail. I've eaten some amazing meat around the world, but nothing compared to what I had in Argentina. I've been there over a dozen times; each time is the same routine: arrive at the hotel in Buenos Aires, go to the steak restaurant, usually my favourite La Brigada or Estilo Campo in Puerto Madero. There I eat a steak the size of a plate and wash it down with Malbec, then pass out until call time. You always know that it will be a great party. All the tours in Argentina sold out and they were all completely rocking until the end.

DJs there are on the same level as rock stars. I once had to change terminals in Buenos Aires Airport with Carl Cox and crew. It was only 200 metres, but the walk took over thirty minutes; Carl stopped for photos with everyone. No doubt he's a recognisable figure anywhere in the electronic music world, but DJs like him are gods down there, in a country where electronic music is a religion for many.

In most Latino countries, the parties are male-dominated, which is the opposite of countries like Russia: at least five men to every woman. Latin countries are mostly still old-fashioned. The men go out a lot, women not so often, so they are far outnumbered. At the big clubs in Argentina like Mandarine Park, which holds twenty thousand people, there is a sea of male faces, with just a few girls dotted in between. The girls need to be tough to survive in there; it can be like a bear pit. The VIP stand is where the beautiful girls hang out at the tables of the wealthy men. This is where the guys on the dance floor dream of being.

Argentina and the Latin countries are full of corruption. Often, when travelling to gigs, we get stopped by the police, who ask for money for no apparent reason, and we have no option but to pay them. One time we were driving down from Buenos Aires to

Mar del Plata, the Argentinian seaside town. Police stopped us on the highway and demanded money to continue. There was no reason at all why we would need to pay them, but we had no choice. We put our pesos together, and they let us continue.

Rival promoters are always playing dirty tricks. They often contact police to report an "illegal party" or "a DJ without an appropriate visa". Police always come down to check, and if they find anything wrong, they will close the party down. Uber drivers drive with their phones hidden next to their seats, fearing that a metered taxi driver will spot them and smash their windows. It's a cut-throat world where nobody trusts anyone.

Around the World in Ten Days

I've heard a lot of mad ideas in my time, but by far the craziest one was when my colleague, Nic Fanciulli, had the idea of going around the world in ten days, playing a gig at every stop. I thought he was joking. Surely it wasn't possible to get around the globe in that short space of time, even without playing gigs. Somehow the idea gained traction and snowballed into reality, and the tour was booked in.

We started it on an Easter weekend, maximising the global holidays. The route went like this: London, Toronto, San Francisco, Tokyo, Manila, Mumbai, Dubai, Madrid, Manchester. Every night, a gig in every city. We lost twenty-four hours flying over time zones. It was effectively nine gigs on nine consecutive nights. One cancelled or missed flight would have brought the tour to a halt. There was no room for any errors.

Nobody had ever attempted a tour like it before, nobody has since, and there is a good reason for that. We had two videographers with us, documenting the whole thing. We had to keep it interesting, or people would switch off. We started off fresh, excited about something so unique. I thought after a few days we would be like the walking dead, going through the motions, but the excitement kept the adrenalin going.

Touring is a fantasy world. Waking up in a new city every day is abnormal. The real world is left behind as soon as you step on that plane; it's like going on holiday every day. Any troubles you encounter are all left behind when you move onto the next destination. Reality often hits you on the day you arrive home, but it's never too long until you are off again.

This tour was not just fantasy; it was a full-on imaginary world — nine different cities with wildly different cultures. Sleeping only on flights, however nice business class is, you never experience the same quality of sleep you get in a hotel bed, as any frequent flyer will tell you.

The only country that was new for me was India. I was excited to go, even just for a day, but paranoid of getting Delhi belly. Eating the local cuisine was all part of the tour, but one wrong choice would have wiped out the tour. The promoter was mindful of this and put us in the Taj Mahal Palace. Guests have included: Queen Elizabeth II, Barack Obama, and Mick Jagger. I ate only in the safety of my room. I wasn't taking any chances in India.

Mumbai was the surprise gig of the tour. It was a Wednesday night at Bluefrog, not a night when people usually go out. We didn't expect much, but the club was packed with excitable people dancing as I've never seen before. It was the first time I realised how popular electronic music is in India and the first time in a while that I saw no sign of pretence or snobbery. The Mumbai crowd literally danced like nobody was watching; the most animated people I have ever seen.

Touching down in Manchester was a huge relief. Incidents always make a good story, but we couldn't afford them here. By far the most punishing ten days of my life, but at the same time, the most exciting. We compared photos from the first day to the last. Gradually, the skin got whiter and the eyes blacker; the mind was working slower but feeling fine. On tour, you can be so shattered that you can hardly speak yet enter a full club, and the tiredness disappears instantly.

The afterparty at the hotel was a celebration of achievement. It felt like we had completed a marathon, a huge feeling of accomplishment mixed with relief. I woke up the next morning in the Manchester hotel room, and I had a text from another DJ. "Are you available to come on tour with me today?" And I was off again. A sucker for punishment. A crazy road warrior.

Sexual Assault in Peru

South America is the hotbed of electronic music. Brazil, Argentina, Colombia I've mentioned already, but many underestimate Peru. Every time, I am blown away by the parties, the people, and especially the food. Peruvian food is exquisite. Without doubt, the best cuisine on the whole continent. When we touch down in Lima, our first stop is always Mercado. The best restaurant in Lima, one of my favourites in the world, and a must when you are in Peru.

As in most of South America, you have to be careful where you go, but be streetwise, and you will be fine. The nightlife is great. It doesn't matter if it's Wednesday or Saturday, it's all the same to the Peruvians. Music and dancing are enshrined in the culture, and electronic music is as big as anything else.

One hour outside Lima is a resort called Asia. It's on the beach, where many locals spend their weekends; it's naturally a place where they party. I've done so many amazing events there. One, in particular, will stay in my mind forever.

It was a huge daytime beach party with people sprawling everywhere. The party stopped just after nightfall, and the beaming promoter invited us to his club. Dubfire took control and played the whole night. At four a.m., I went for a break outside.

Two beautiful Peruvian girls, one blonde, one brunette, both pretty drunk, got chatting to me. One, who I called "The Boss," lived in Miami and was back visiting family; the other one was the innocent girl next door. It was soon clear which one made the decisions. My Spanish is basic, but I understood. "We are taking him home."

I pretended not to hear but wondered what they were planning.

They conferred a bit more, then The Boss gave the orders, and they both jumped on me, kissing me all over my face and neck. I saw eyes around me staring; it was quite a sight. People wondered what I had. I had no idea. I was pretty shocked, but I didn't put up a fight. This was Peru, not Vegas. I had never seen sluts like this before.

I told them we had to stop. This was not the place. "*Vamos*," they replied. My hotel was behind the club. Dubfire was in no mood to stop; he had the whole club rocking, so I left him alone. The girls escorted me outside, arm in arm, hanging off me, lipstick all over my face like a clown. I had no idea why I was their chosen one. They were on a mission. Nothing was going to stop them. I was their victim.

We walked through the busy party streets, their long legs staggering on their heels like Bambi on ice.

The hotel was just a few minutes' walk, but it was a true walk of shame. Everyone was staring at the show.

We arrived at the hotel. The sun was already coming up. I hadn't even walked into my room, and they were both stripped off. Was this really happening? The Boss was giving orders like a madam in a whorehouse. She had been corrupted in the School of Miami and was showing her girl how it was done. Not so innocent any more, the blondie followed, curious and in fear of her mentor.

It was a wild session in my room. I woke up hungover with a girl on either side. We all started laughing. It turned out that The Boss was married with two kids in Miami. Blondie was single but on the road to no good.

We all keep in touch and even meet up when I'm back in town. No more antics; they're actually very nice people. A crazy way to meet friends, you might think, but this is tour life, and you must be open to anything, especially two pairs of hot Peruvian legs at the same time.

Scandinavian Strip Search

I love Scandinavia: good people, very polite, everything works well; I really don't go there often enough. Electronic music didn't catch on there the same as the rest of Europe. Surprising, as so much amazing music comes out of this region of famously creative people.

My first time in Norway, it was my birthday, and I was excited to go to the country of Vikings, salmon and fjords. I flew into Oslo Gardermoen alone. My friends were picking me up from the airport and would show me the sights. I walked through the sleek Scandinavian airport, through passport control, and I was on my way. Well, at least I thought I was.

I felt a tap on the shoulder. "Come with me, sir."

I was taken to a room and interrogated. He was an undercover police officer. Everything I said didn't go down well. I was travelling alone, playing music, only staying for the weekend. He wasn't impressed.

"Do you sell drugs?" he asked.

"No, I do not."

"Take off your clothes."

I had travelled through airports every week of my life, taken thousands of flights, but I had never been stopped by anyone, let alone strip-searched. He was serious. I was soon in my birthday suit.

He took my clothes, shoes, and everything else away. I stood there, completely naked, in a room of one-way mirrors, cameras staring at me from all corners. I started getting nervous, thinking they could plant something or even find something that I had no idea was there. It was a nervous wait. The guy eventually came back.

"You can get dressed and go. Welcome to Norway."

I wasn't going to leave it there. I asked him why he had singled me out in an airport of hundreds of arriving passengers. "We have many people coming here from London to sell drugs," he said. "You fitted the description."

I walked out two hours after my flight had arrived. My friends had left, thinking I wasn't coming. My phone had stopped working since the police had gone through it. I got a taxi into Oslo, no longer excited about my trip. Nothing makes you feel as low as being forced to strip naked in front of a stranger. I did the gig and left next day. I was in no rush to return. The promoter contacted me six months later. "We would like you to come back," he said. I accepted, but in the back of my mind, I was worried.

I landed in Oslo once again. I went nervously through passport control and couldn't believe it. There he was, the same guy. He had much less hair than the year before, but I recognised the big blue eyes. I tried walking ahead, pretending not to see him, but he walked over and tapped me again. "Come with me."

I asked if he recognised me.

"No."

I told him that he had searched me just six months before. Perhaps he stripped off so many people that he couldn't remember who.

"Did I find any drugs?"

"No, of course not," I replied.

"Take off your clothes."

This time, I refused. I told him that I would prefer to fly back to London rather than be strip-searched again if that was an option. He went out and came back.

"OK," he said. "I'll pat you down and take your shoes, and you can keep your clothes on unless I find anything."

I took it. I wasn't being stripped again, and if I had flown back to London, I would have cancelled the gig. He found nothing, and I was free to go. Another bad arrival to Norway, which stayed in my mind the whole weekend. I returned one year later for a third time, nervous again, but this time the guy wasn't there, and I sailed through without any hassle. Hopefully, he had been fired for stripping off the wrong people. I've travelled through thousands of airports since then and never been searched. Somehow Oslo is the place that always targets me.

Ibiza — The Changing Island

My first time in Ibiza was on holiday in 1995. I've been every year since then and survived four whole summer seasons. The Ibiza we see nowadays is very different from how it was back then: the hippie vibes, the hedonism, the friendliness and openness of the people. VIP tables didn't exist. Everyone was equal. It didn't matter what your job was or how much money you had; everyone was on the same level.

I remember the dance floor at Space, Kate Moss on the one side of me and a taxi driver on the other. It was amazing — a leveller like nowhere else — everyone from different backgrounds, all dancing as one, to the same music, shoulder to shoulder without a care in the world.

Those days are well and truly over; the island is now marketed mostly towards the wealthy jet-set clientele. VIPs are kept totally separate from the rest of the riff-raff. Tables costing up to €20,000 are bought by clueless guys who know nothing about music. Middle Eastern oil barons and Russian oligarchs compete over who has the biggest bottle, with their aggressive private security guards, which kills the vibe.

With that comes the price hikes. €25 for a vodka limone? Many real clubbers have shunned it for cheaper alternatives. The island still has some magic. Cova Santa, DC10 and Underground keep the old vibe alive, where you can find free-spirited souls. Ushuaïa and Destino are the only open-air clubs that remain. Both are very good, but over by eleven p.m.

Ibiza afterparties are a thing of the past. First-timers don't believe me. "It's Ibiza, parties non-stop, right?" Wrong. At six a.m., my phone always buzzes with messages. "Where is the after?"

Afters start at five p.m. the next day. What kind of afterparty is that? It's a whole new party, surely. What can we do until then? Unless you know someone with a villa, you have no options. The "party capital of the world" has fewer options than Zürich.

Ibiza is crime ridden. You'll find it hard to meet one person with a villa who hasn't been robbed. It happened to me several times: cash, phones, laptops, it's a whole economy. The police do nothing. Many say they work with the gangs, not against them.

Another dark economy is importing women. I see beautiful girls flown in by sponsors — guys who they've never met before. On landing, they'll be whisked away from the airport to a private villa and taken to VIP clubs. Fuelled with drugs, often without knowing, there is only one outcome at the end of the night. If they don't put out, they will be replaced the next day. A table at Pacha costs an average monthly wage; for these women, there is no other way to see the island. If you see a beautiful girl in Ibiza, it's too good to be true. She's not "on holiday with the girls" — someone, somewhere, will be financing it.

There are so many other options now: Greece, Croatia, Malta, Romania. Beautiful places with strong party scenes. Mykonos recently emerged as a major contender but is aimed at the same jet-set crowd, prices even higher. Yet, Ibiza still has something. There is magic if you look hard. The beauty and charm of the island will never go away. Just be seated when you read your credit card bill when you arrive home.

I could write a separate book on Ibiza stories, but that's been done before. It's an island where many arrive and discover the animal inside them if they didn't already know. Most of my wildest nights were at the Ibiza Gran Hotel. The first five-star hotel in Ibiza, it raised the bar. A stone's throw away from Pacha and Marina Botafoc, all rooms are equipped with jacuzzis, terraces and full twenty-four-hour bars. It was the perfect place to finish the night. We started the night on stage at Ushuaïa, peak time in August at ANTS, and two of my DJs were playing; they asked me to invite some girls. It was one of those weeks when I knew no-one in town. I told them to forget about girls unless they wanted to pay, but they were hungry. They didn't know anyone, so they were banking on me. There were only two hours left, and on stage, there were only guys. Suddenly, I received a message. "Hey, Ross, are you in

Ibiza? I'm here with my girls. We want to come to Ushuaïa."

You know that final sequence of *Dumb and Dumber* with the bus full of girls? That's what it felt like. It was a girl I know from Miami, the only girl I knew who came to Ibiza unsponsored. She had six of her girlfriends. I took them up to the stage. The DJs' faces lit up.

Miami girls party hard. Within thirty minutes, our drinks rider was gone. At the end of the night, we crammed into the van and went back to the hotel. I had an early flight the next day. An afterparty was not a good idea. I dropped them off and went back to my room next door. I tried to fall asleep, but the loud music and laughing kept me awake. I was smiling; they were getting some action. These girls were from Miami — there was no doubt about that.

Suddenly, my phone buzzed continuously. Someone needed a lighter. I don't even smoke, but I tend to keep useful things. I was half asleep. I floated down the corridor in just my shorts, the sound of girls' voices getting louder. I knocked on the door, but I didn't want to go in. One of the girls answered, half-naked. "Ross, come in," she said. I walked in, and it was like a playboy mansion. The guys were snorting cocaine off the half-naked girls. The jacuzzi was full and almost overflowing with the amount of water (and girls) inside. I told them to be careful and walked back out. It was messy and only three hours until call time. I woke up at six thirty for the flight, I called the DJ's room, and a faint voice answered. "Can you come here? I have a problem."

I walked into his room. Inside was like a scene from a Tarantino movie: girls passed out everywhere, empty bottles, lines, cigarette ash and under three centimetres of water. We abandoned the scene and went to the airport; it was only one hour until the flight. We didn't hear anything from the hotel until late afternoon when there was an email: five thousand euros room damage and room service costs. That was one expensive afterparty.

Take Ibiza for what it is. You don't get value for money, but you will still find a beautiful island with mostly positive people. I hope it will go back to how it was before, with less red tape and more open-air events with the free-spirit vibe. The Ibiza council are ruining the island with the way they are running it. I'm confident that it will return to being the undisputed best party place in the world, as it was for so long.

The Way to Roll in the USA

Halloween is my favourite time of the year, and the USA is the best place to spend it. People go to unbelievable lengths, especially the girls. It's the one time of the year they can dress like a slut and it's accepted. I've spent three Halloweens in the USA. Two in New York, but nothing beats Hollywood. A perfect set for a costumed cast, the streets are closed to traffic due to so many people, all dressed up.

My colleague and I arrived in L.A., hungover from the night before. On tour, you take one day as it comes. Halloween costumes are at the back of your mind. "Don't worry," our friend said, "I got it covered."

Sound in L.A. is my favourite club in the USA, owned by Kobi, an old friend. We met in the hotel lobby for some pre-drinks. Our friends arrived with two costumes: Batman and Robin. We squabbled over who would take the cool Batman outfit. I lost. I put on the Robin costume. I looked like a buffoon. Fuck it — it's Halloween.

Kobi texted me: "The car is outside." He'd sent a Rolls Royce Phantom. We jumped in and cruised through the *closed* streets of Hollywood. The police saw the car and paved the way, no questions asked. Tens of thousands of people filled the streets, every costume you can imagine. The Batmobile pulled up outside the club, and there was a huge line of people. It was like a casting for *Captain Marvel*. We opened the doors in sync and got out to a huge roar from the crowd. We had stolen the show before the club even opened.

As far as fun goes, you can't beat Halloween. It's impossible to be serious. The USA is one of the most superficial countries on earth, but at Halloween, the fakeness is left at the door.

A Sunny Place for Shady People

The first place I ever played in the USA was Miami, back in 2006. The Miami Music Conference, later known as Miami Music Week, was a big fixture in the calendar back in the day. Miami is one of the most famous cities in the world, a truly global party capital. Perfect for a DJ hoping to crack America. I dreamed of going there, but what a disappointment.

The hostile immigration at Miami airport was the first encounter. I thought America and Britain were supposed to be friends. You would never think that. The guy went right through my passport, questioning every single stamp. "What were you doing in the United Arab Emirates?" He barked at me like a US marine.

"I was on holiday. Why?"

It was clear that he had seen the word "Arab" and thought I might be a terrorist. His name badge read "Sanchez," which was quite ironic. After countless more questions, he eventually let me in. I thought Miami was a tourist hotspot; why were they so hostile?

After one day, things were not quite right. Things that people told me mostly never happened. People were tricky, shifty, lying through their teeth. The good people I met were mostly the Europeans. One of them explained it to me. "Miami is a city of chancers, mostly from Latin America. They will tell you anything. It's a sunny place for shady people."

The more time I spend in Miami, the more I see that it's true. I love Latin American people, but something happens to many of them when they get to Miami. Slippery promoters, devious culture. Beneath that paradise, there is a murky world.

I somehow got used to it. Nowhere in the world is perfect. Take the rough with the smooth. Miami is paradise, but you need to stay on your guard. It's the party capital of the USA. One of the only cities where clubs can serve alcohol after two a.m. It's definitely worth a trip, but not for long periods. There are some good honest promoters, who we tend to exclusively work with these days, but they are always European

No Time for Fakes

I've already said that I love the USA, but the fake people get to me. It took a few tours to get it, but eventually, the cultural differences hit you.

Many years ago, I dreamed of a new watch. The Panerai Luminor was the one, a classic DJ's watch, which would set me back $10,000. It remained just a dream. I was walking through Patpong market on my last day in Bangkok, and there it was: the Panerai Luminor. Except it was fifty bucks. "Same, same, but different," the little Thai man said. It looked like the real deal. I negotiated him down to forty dollars, very pleased with my counterfeit bargain.

Two weeks later, I was flying to the USA on American Airlines. "That's a beautiful watch, sir," the flight attendant said. This was the moment I realised that people in the USA look for materialistic things. Nobody had noticed it in Europe beforehand.

Three dates into the tour, we arrived in Ontario, Canada. Same, same but different. Canadians love to say that they are different from Americans, but I believe they are much the same. Canadian closing time is also a draconian two a.m., so we went back to the promoter's house after the club. "Hey, guys, what would you like to drink?" he asked. "My wife will make them for you."

I'm a simple guy; I just drink what's on offer.

"I have this red wine," his wife said said, showing us the bottle.

"Honey! Do you think a guy with a watch like that would drink cheap wine? Give him the reserve!"

I laughed out loud; they had no idea why. I was wearing a watch that was cheaper than the bottle, but it highlighted how superficial people could be.

Six months later, the watch stopped working. It might have fooled the promoter, but it was a piece of shit inside. I finally bought a real Panerai, which I still have to this day, and yes, I only receive comments in the USA and Canada.

The USA, despite its downsides, is still one of my favourite countries to go to. I spent the best month of my life there, and the second, third and fourth too. So many things are broken: the politics, the superficial society, the gun problems, school shootings — I could go on and on, but I focus on the positives. There are enough to keep me going back again and again. It's one of the most welcoming countries in the world; there are some real characters who I find very entertaining. Some are just whacked-out, others just confident. You'll never meet a shy American. Positive, loud, and love to party. A perfect country for DJs on tour.

Losing It

One of the biggest downsides of touring is losing your things. Every night, a different hotel, it's a recipe for leaving stuff behind. Never use the safe in the hotel — it's asking for trouble. Many DJs get to the airport after a gig, then realise that they've left their passport in the safe. One DJ I toured with had a pair of shoes that he would only wear in the daytime, one of which he would keep in the safe with his passport. Those few minutes that you have in the morning before pick-up, it's so easy to forget things, but if you have one shoe in the safe, you won't forget anything that's with it.

I always keep my things together in one corner. Once you start dotting them around your hotel room, inevitably, you will lose them. I haven't lost much, considering the number of gigs I've done, but the one time I did, it spiralled out of hand.

I was flying from Stockholm to Amsterdam, where I had a connection to Paraguay for a two-week South America tour. It was an early seven a.m. flight. I did some work on the plane, then put my MacBook Air in the seat pocket in front, took a Xanax and went to sleep. Two hours later, I woke up in Schiphol. A bit disorientated, I got off the plane and through passport control. Fuck, I'd left my laptop on the plane.

I went to the info desk, and they called the gate. It would be a few hours before any lost property was handed in. I had three hours before my flight to Asunción. A two-week tour without my laptop would be a disaster. Why do these things always happen when you are going away? That MacBook was my life; all of my music, my emails, and my photos were in there. Swedes and the Dutch are honest people. Surely someone would hand it in.

I stood next to the info desk the whole time. Eventually, the lady gave me the news. Nothing had been found. I couldn't believe it. I was sure someone would hand it in. Of all the flights to leave my laptop on, it was the one before such a long tour. I wouldn't have the chance to buy one at the airport; my flight was almost boarding.

It was a long flight to Paraguay. No laptop, no emails, no Netflix. I can't watch the in-flight movies. The sound quality is bad, they cut the best bits out, I end up just switching off. Something in my mind told me that I would land and receive a message that my laptop had been found.

I landed, but no news. The next few days were non-stop: Rio, Buenos Aires, Lima, Medellin. No time to go shopping. I called Schiphol airport every day, just in case. The lady started to recognise my voice. I asked where the plane had flown to after Amsterdam, but she told me it didn't matter. As it was KLM Airlines, any lost property would always be taken to Schiphol, without exception. I had to take her word for it.

One week later, and I had still no news. Trying to work on a phone for two weeks is almost impossible. I had one day off in Rio. I went to the Apple Store — closed for holidays. It was not my tour. In the back of my mind, I still had a feeling that my MacBook would be found.

I checked the flight stat websites. I saw that the plane had flown on to Gran Canaria after Amsterdam. I called Las Palmas Airport from my hotel in Rio. It was late at night there. A quiet female voice answered. "Yes, we have a MacBook here," she said. My heart started racing. "Can you prove that it's yours?" Mine looked the same as anyone else's, nothing different. She asked for my password. I hesitated for a while. Giving my password away to a random stranger was not a good idea, but I had nothing to lose. She entered the password. I heard that magic Apple log in sound. It was the one. Result!

I asked if she could send it on the next flight to Amsterdam. "No," was the straight answer. Surely it couldn't be that difficult to send a laptop back to the place it had come from, especially as the airline policy was to hold it in Schiphol. She wouldn't post it either. "If you want your laptop back, you must come here yourself," she said.

I told her that I was in Rio, and it would take some time. I don't think she believed me, but she said she would hold it for one more week.

I finished the tour. It was the last day in Medellin, and I was running on empty. No energy, no laptop. I took the usual route back. Medellin — Bogota — Madrid. I bought a new flight from Madrid to Las Palmas. The flight was delayed. It was a long afternoon at Madrid Airport and an even longer flight. I had forgotten how far down the Canary Islands are, next to the Sahara Desert.

I finally landed. I was pretty braindead. My watch said midnight, the time that Lost Property closed, but we had gone back one hour since Madrid. It was actually eleven p.m.; still time. It was the last flight in; the airport was dead, not a soul around. I found Lost Property, but it was closed. I went to the info desk, and a sleepy woman looked up. I explained the story; she looked impressed that I had travelled so far from Colombia for a laptop. She grabbed some keys and took me to the office, but there was no laptop anywhere. "Sorry," she said. "Your Mac isn't here."

I couldn't believe it. I had travelled so far. Gran Canaria was not the place I wanted to be on a dark rainy night at the end of October and all for nothing. We walked out of the office, and I sat in the airport café, which was now closed. There was a flight home at six a.m. No point in going to a hotel now. There were none at the airport, only far away.

A homeless man walked in and made his bed next to me, followed by another, then another. After one hour, I was surrounded by tramps. The smell was awful. Just one day before, I was on a South American DJ tour, and now I was sleeping rough with *vagabundos*. I had to get out of there. I walked back to the info desk to ask about a hotel. "Oh, there you are," the same sleepy lady said. I had stirred her again. "I was looking for you." She had called her colleague who works in Lost Property; she had hidden it in her private safe. She took me back to the office, and there it was. My MacBook. I gave her a hug; I was so relieved. I had just three hours until my flight. I went back to the café with the homeless. I didn't care any more; I had a thousand emails to catch up on. I never left anything on a flight after that; it was an extreme lesson learnt. I never left anything on a plane after that.

Dangerous Women

Clubland has a lot of pitfalls. Drugs, alcohol, toxic people, but the biggest one for me is dangerous women.

I've never seen so many escort girls in clubs as I do these days. It's become industry standard. Electronic music used to be about a club of sweaty ravers in a dark room. Since the glam crept in, so has the brass. In places like Milan, Marbella, Dubai, you see them everywhere. I'm at the point now where I don't talk to girls in clubs; there is a ninety per cent chance that they will be on the game. As my friend told me recently, "When a guy wakes up with a hangover in Dubai, he will say 'I partied hard; I'm $10,000 down.' When a girl wakes up in Dubai, she will say 'I partied hard; I'm $10,000 up.'"

I don't have anything against prostitutes, as long as they are open about it. What gets me is when they disguise themselves as "normal girls", then hit you with the surprise at the end of the night.

Many start as image girls — girls who are paid just to be in the club and party. Their job is just to smile and flirt so that the guys feel good and buy more bottles. In most cases, they are very cool, smart, good-looking, intelligent girls and many are in university. They didn't quite make it as models, but they look good in the club.

Flights and accommodation are paid for by the clubs. For a young girl looking to travel the world, it can be a nice little lifestyle.

Guys arriving at places such as Ibiza or Marbella can call agencies who send them catalogues of girls, and they take their pick. You'll see a big table in a restaurant, ten places at the table but only five guys sitting, the seats between them vacant. A van of beautiful girls pulls up, and they take the empty seats. Then they continue with dinner like they have known each other all their lives. After two hours is up, the girls leave the table and go to their next booking; the guys are alone again.

Image girls have become standard in clubland. They are as much part of the club as the DJs, but it's a fine line between this and escorting. Guys who pay beautiful girls for their company don't like it when they are suddenly taken away. Naturally, more money will be offered, and when the amount gets high, it can be difficult to turn down. Often as DJs, the only girls we know are image girls. They are paid to be around — sometimes the only girls in the club.

One friend of mine is an Ibiza image girl. She earns a very basic wage, €150 a night — not even enough to pay rent in Ibiza. She told me that she had started charging guys for her company. "That's escorting," I said.

"No, escorting is when you have sex with the guy."

I disagreed. Escorting, surely, is payment for services, whether it be sex or company or whatever. One day we met up at a beach club in Ibiza; I could tell that she had something to get off her chest. She had met with a guy for dinner, a notorious old Swiss banker who comes to Ibiza every summer to spend his hard-earned cash on women.

I'd heard so much about him. He had offered her €10,000 for sex. She asked me what she should do as she was struggling to make ends meet. "Don't do it," I said. Ibiza is a very small island. People who live there find out everything. "If you need to borrow money, just ask me." She told me that she wouldn't do it.

One week later, she posted photos online from the beautiful Swiss mountains, of brand-new designer clothes and bags. I even recognised the chalet from other girls' posts who he had invited there. She had succumbed to the temptations, which I see so many other girls do. She came back to Ibiza, but we never spoke again. An example of a good girl coming to Ibiza and leaving as a whore. I've seen it countless times; the temptations are too great for some. Money talks, but so should morals. It's difficult when you can't make ends meet, but there are more dignified ways to make money.

Instagram is where the covers are blown. Girls can't resist posting their whole lives; it's where everything is revealed. So many Instagram "models" who don't appear to have any work are always posting photos on luxury yachts and villas. Who is paying for all of this is the first instinct.

As I said before, DJing can be a lonely life, sitting in the hotel alone, waiting to be picked up. Suddenly you receive a message from a girl who wants to come to the party. "Can you put me on the guest list?" How can you say no?

When Instagram introduced messaging, I knew we were doomed. It started as an innocent photo app; now it's more like Tinder, with girls looking for that sugar daddy. DJs are one of the targets.

I've seen evidence of girls sending DJs naked photos of themselves, asking if they can accompany him to his gig, even if it's in another country. One DJ I know hooks up regularly with girls on Instagram and flies them out to his gigs every weekend, a different one every time. If they arrive and they don't look as good as they do in their photos, he sends them back home. It's a crazy way to live but highlights what a lonely life it can be, where the only people you can meet are Instagram randoms.

I'll never forget one time in L.A., undoubtedly, home of some of the most dangerous women in the world. The owner of the club - Kobi invited me to his bar in the afternoon for a drink. I went down and joined him.

I was standing talking; two girls were behind, sitting, chatting but looking at me. One of the girls, who was wearing a dress, literally opened her legs, pulled her pants to the side and showed me her pussy. I tried to continue talking as normal, but it was difficult to keep a straight face, so I told him what she had done. He turned around, but she crossed her legs and continued talking as normal, pretending that nothing had happened at all.

"Ross, it's normal here. L.A. is full of sluts, be careful." It turned out to be one of the best pieces of advice I've ever been given. I've seen similar behaviour every time, but that was the most audacious.

One question that many people ask me is: "Oh, you are a DJ; do you have a girlfriend in every country?" It's one of the most annoying questions ever and totally not true. As I mentioned earlier, DJing is one of the loneliest professions around. In the clubs, DJs are working and not able to speak to anyone. The bigger DJs play until the end of the night when most people are going home. The average guy going to a club will meet far more people than the DJ, so why people believe that we meet a lot of girls compared to everyone else in the club baffles me. We are in a country almost always for one night. No chance to meet a girlfriend, let alone one in every country.

I remember the times of "DJ groupies" hanging around the booth, but they are almost extinct these days. It's more worthwhile for them to hang out in VIP areas where they can meet wealthy guys and drink champagne. By the time we get to the club, they have usually found what they want, far away from the stage.

Many guys ask me, "Where are the easiest women in the world?" Always from the English-speaking countries: the USA, the UK, Australia, New Zealand, Ireland, Canada, South Africa... any country where English is the mother tongue. Perhaps it's the trash TV that creates the culture; it's the only explanation I've found. I've heard many DJs say, "I haven't got laid in a while, but I have a US tour coming soon."

I always get asked where are the most beautiful women. Undoubtedly, Russia, Ukraine and Belarus. Who knows what's in the water there, but be particularly careful of dangerous women. I've learnt the hard way, trust me.

Pitfalls of the Scene

Avicii's death highlighted the scene's problems with drugs and alcohol. Many people have attempted or committed suicide due to the stresses of tour life; Avicii was a prime example. Many of us could already see what was going to happen to him, but it was ironic that he died long after he had retired from DJing. He was being pushed into performing by those around him who were on his payroll, even though he was often not in any kind of state even to stand up.

Most of us have a "show must go on" attitude, whereby we will continue however sick we are, but the death of Avicii made many of us in the scene reflect on our lifestyle and be more careful with our health. The day that he died, I was on tour in Argentina. When I heard the news, I was sad but not shocked. The years of touring had taken their toll on him. His mental state was at the point where he just couldn't continue. Even one year after retiring from the decks, he still hadn't mentally recovered.

His death was a pivotal moment for those of us in the music industry, especially those who were touring so heavily, and many of us took a good look at what we were doing. In my case, I asked myself the question, what was more important — the shows or our health.

Keith Flint from The Prodigy was the biggest shock to me. Arguably the best front man of any dance act ever, he also decided to end his life while he seemed to have the world at his feet. The moment I found out I just sat there with my head in my hands for hours, then went and blasted one of his tracks as loud as I could and danced around as he would have wanted.

In 2020, Erick Morillo took his own life. He had his own battles, different demons. At one stage, he was the number one DJ in the world — the undisputed king of House music. Then drugs got involved, and his career spiralled. Eventually, he died on the eve of a court appearance. I know how this feels, having been there myself. The thought of suicide did cross my mind. I wasn't cut out for jail, but I knew I was innocent and decided to fight on. It could have gone either way. Who knows what was going through his mind?

The intense travel of touring has an adverse effect on the body and overall health. It's not normal to be taking so many flights per week, spending nights in loud, crowded nightclubs, grabbing fast food on the go, drinking alcohol to keep you going and whatever else people choose to take. Ultimately, this is going to cause damage. I always exercised at least twice a week to keep my body fit to withstand the intense lifestyle, but I have still had my problems. Many DJs don't exercise at all which I think is a mistake.

The Rules of Touring

There are many things that you learn while touring that become unwritten rules. In many cases, I've learnt the hard way.

First, never check in bags. We are in new countries every day. If the airline loses your bag, it will follow you around the world and never catch you up until you arrive home. You have to learn to travel light — everything into hand luggage, even for one-month tours.

Always wear ear plugs. I learnt the hard way. I didn't wear them for years, constantly exposed to loud, harsh sound systems. You know that ringing noise you have at the end of the night, and when you wake up, it's gone? One day I woke up, and it hadn't gone. It stayed with me forever and became the soundtrack of my life, even to this day. When I am in a quiet room, it drives me mad. Vicious ringing that never stops, and there is no cure. I protect my ears now, but the damage is done. I still see many DJs and crew not wearing plugs, with extremely loud monitors. I only wish that they don't end up like me. I recommend anyone who spends time in clubs, working or otherwise, to wear ear plugs.

Always have a positive attitude. Touring is hard. You will have cancelled flights, driver no-shows, many people will let you down, you'll have good gigs and bad. Sleep deprivation leads to low energy levels. However much it affects you, always stay positive. There are never problems, only solutions. If you have a bad gig, start the new day with a clean slate — no need for grudges or bad moods. The only way is forward.

Set numerous alarms. The consequences of missed flights are too high. On tour, you are lucky to get three hours' sleep at a time. Cancelled gigs are an expensive mess. Always set at least four alarms and an additional hotel wake up call. If one doesn't wake you, the other one will.

Always give good energy to everyone. Nobody cares where you have been the night before, if you slept or not, how far you travelled. Once you arrive, they want one hundred per cent from you. The fans pay good money to come to the gigs. Never let them down, always be professional, and always be polite.

Take at least two of everything in two different bags: phone, passport, cables, credit cards, et cetera. Inevitably these will get lost or stolen. Being stuck in the middle of nowhere with no money or phone is not fun. I've had everything stolen on tour.

Don't become phoney like the people around you. There are many fake people in music. Keep your standards and morals high. Stay on the ground, and don't let the fakes convert you.

Be very careful what you post on social media, especially if you've had a drink and are not thinking straight. Social media is rife with trolls — sick-minded people who take pleasure from bringing people's careers down. I've seen it happen to some of my colleagues who innocently posted something for fun, not thinking straight, but were taken down by these twisted characters. Usually bitter failed DJs themselves, they are very tough behind their screens, yet if you confront them in real life, they run a mile. It's so easy to post something while in the touring fantasy world, then, next day, realise that it didn't quite please the twisted trolls looking for their agendas. I hate social media. Touring was so much more fun without it. These days whatever you do, someone is pointing a phone camera at you and can't wait for a reason to bring you down — bitter, twisted people who are jealous of your success. Sometimes I wonder what this decade is we are living in.

Finally, and most importantly, don't clap when the plane lands. This should be outlawed.

Master Blaggers

One thing that annoys me the most is what we call blaggers: People who believe that they are entitled to free entry, free drinks for themselves and all of their friends, for no legitimate reason.

I receive messages from people who I haven't spoken to for years. "Hey, Ross, how's it going? Hope you are good. Please can you put me on the guest list for Ibiza this weekend?" Sometimes for parties that I am nothing to do with. I don't mind if they are actually real friends or if they work in the music industry, but many of them are just blaggers.

A DJ only gets ten guests on his list. I'll get messages: "Can you put me, plus ten?" No names. They don't even know who the ten will be. I try to accommodate everyone I can, but if I tell them no, the sulks and tantrums start.

As far as guest list requests go, Ibiza is the worst. The ticket prices are so high. People get desperate; they try anything not to pay. Once they are inside, the drink prices are so high that they don't want to pay for them either. Our drinks rider gets raided. I have to hide it every time.

Blaggers are a global thing. You will find them everywhere. I was arriving at the BPM Festival in Portugal. Two Chilean guys were waiting at the back entrance, possibly had been for hours. They snuck in behind me as the security shut the gate so that they looked like they were with me — slick operation. I didn't even see them until it was too late. They followed me through the festival, right up to the stage, then tried to come into the booth. I said, "Look, guys, I've got you backstage, but you can't come to the booth; it's DJs only." You'd swear I had killed someone with the reaction I got.

These are master blaggers, people who we don't even know, waiting outside the party for us to arrive and follow us in. The host will assume that anyone behind the DJ is part of his group. Often I am already inside before I realise that we are with completely random people, and it's too late. The cheek of them is quite staggering.

If you tell them that they have to leave the stage, they will try the charm. "Bro, I love your music. You are amazing; please, can I stay?" This makes it more difficult to kick them out. If they are female, they start flirting and smiling, trying to melt us into letting them in. I stopped falling for that.

The USA wins the title for the most professional blaggers. Miami, New York, and L.A. are at the top of the league. These people could talk their way into the White House. I get people coming up to me telling me that they need to be backstage. They always sound credible. I believed them in my young naïve days and let them in, but since then, I've learnt to spot a fake a mile away.

I came across the biggest blagger at Avalon Hollywood, one of the best clubs in L.A. California is yet another state with a backwards law where you can't buy alcohol after two a.m. Avalon, however, is unique. It has a twenty-four-hour licence and stays open throughout the night, but there's no booze after two a.m. The bar opens again at six a.m. It's a ridiculous rule, as all people do for those four hours is get wired on drugs. Everything becomes dark for those four hours, both the venue and the mood. Only the smart DJs know how to sense the crowd and play the right sound to catch the vibe.

It was around 05.50, and a dreadlocked guy came in from the back of the stage with a microphone in his hand.

"Hey, I'm the club MC. I'm here to announce the bar opening."

It was an unusual thing to ask, but he looked the part and had the mic ready to plug in. I told him to go ahead. He plugged in his mic and started to rap. He was very good. The clock turned six; he announced that the bar was open, MC-style. People rushed to the bar, ordering catch up shots, the whole vibe lifted. He was rocking it.

"Who the fuck is that?" I heard from behind me. It was the owner.

"I thought he was one of your guys?"

"I've never seen his face before. Get him out!"

Two huge guards came. He quickly pulled out his microphone and was hauled out of the club. I had been totally duped. This was Hollywood. The best actors in the world, and the fakest of all places. This guy had talent. I hope he got his break somewhere. I had learnt a lesson myself. Don't trust anyone in L.A. clubs. Master blaggers.

Living in the 'Dam

It was 2017. I had lived in London, Barcelona and Sydney. I was looking for somewhere new. When you can base yourself anywhere with an airport and internet connection, the world is your oyster. My mind never settles, always thinking of new places to explore and live. The UK had just voted to leave the EU; I felt like I should make the most of it while I could.

Amsterdam is the electronic music capital of the world. Berlin and London might disagree, but no other country has as many events per capita as the Netherlands. The Amsterdam Dance Event is the pinnacle of the dance music calendar; anyone who is anyone is there. Meetings are held here, which decide the whole future annual calendar of global events, and the ADE parties are as good as anywhere. Friends of mine in London, who I live down the road from, who I never see, say, "Let's meet at ADE?" I may as well just live there.

I've been going to the 'Dam since I was a child. I love Dutch people: The most welcoming, friendly, happy people I have ever met. Especially helpful when you don't speak a word of the language.

They are the most open-minded people; nothing shocks them, and everything is acceptable. Schiphol Airport is one of the best transport hubs and only fifteen minutes from the centre. For someone who works in electronic music and travels a lot, it's *the* best place to live.

I moved to De Pijp. A vibey neighbourhood and food mecca. Every second building, a cool restaurant or bar; it's as cosmopolitan as it gets. Then you have the coffee shops. There is one on every street in Amsterdam; the smell of weed always in the air. I had a great one on my doorstep. Sitting on my terrace was like a comedy show. Groups of tourists walking in, leaving one hour later, out of their minds on Fleur's space cakes, laughing uncontrollably and falling over. I'd see them staggering down the street, then go back around the block in circles, totally lost.

I would live in the parallel touring universe on the weekend and return to a different one during the week. It was a full-time fantasy world. There is no city in the world more fun than Amsterdam. Friends would come and visit almost every week. My place was overflowing during ADE. DJs, agents, managers, and friends would stay at mine as the city's hotels and B&Bs were fully booked. The local dealer had my address on auto, but I never met him myself. Every week I would have pills, weed and all kind of leftover powder deposited in my flat before people flew out. The stash mounting higher and higher. Pills in every shape, from Donald Trump to love hearts. The word was spreading, and afterparties at mine were getting popular.

I would arrive home from tour absolutely shattered, but new people would be arriving. I lived next to the Museum Quarter. Nobody was interested. To this day, I have never been to a museum in Amsterdam. Everyone who came to visit only wanted the same things: weed, the red-light district, space cakes, magic mushrooms. That was it. I would arrive from tour totally shattered, needing to sleep for days, but ending up in a coffee shop ordering cakes and babysitting first-timers on mushrooms.

I would do the same and join in the fun (and it really was fun), but eventually, I had to stop. I was living in the most fun, liberal, open-minded city in the world, it was great, but it was too much. Seven days a week without giving the body a break was taking its toll.

I still had friends visiting most weeks. They expected me to join the action, but I would take them out, show them where to go and leave them to it. They were shocked that I, the party man in their eyes, didn't want to get involved any more. They would come back totally high, often their first time, many unable to deal with it. When you are wasted on mushrooms, you can't stay indoors. I have lost count of how many times I have walked around Vondelpark — more laps than Max Verstappen — holding people's hands, telling them everything will be OK, talking them through their hallucinations until they passed out. Eventually, I had to limit the visitors. It was all too much. When you are hard touring, you need to relax when you are at home.

So many mad, mad things happened in Amsterdam. The most fun times I've ever had. It's the Bangkok of Europe. Anything goes. I could have stayed my whole life there; I felt like I had finally found my place, but winter had arrived, and a new opportunity came: Asia.

Paradise Turned Suicide

It was 2019. I had spent New Year in Tokyo then onto Vietnam. Epizode Festival in Phu Quoc is the best place to spend the New Year. I had gigs with two DJs in Phuket: Fanciulli and Dubfire, with a few weeks in between. I decided to spend the whole winter in Asia. I never liked cold winters anyway.

I've been going to Thailand since 2003. First as a backpacker, then for holidays, then many times for work. It's my favourite place to spend winters, escaping bleak Europe. I would be alone this time, but like always, I would make it work. I have friends there I had met while touring; I could continue to work remotely while I was there.

I have always loved Thailand. I love the people: extremely humble, respectful, genuine, and Thai food is my number one. The lull in the events scene in January means it's the best time to take holidays, and Thailand has been my preferred location to spend it in the last few years.

The first few weeks were perfect. Our friends at Circoloco did their first party at Baba Beach Club; it was something special. Exactly what Thailand needed to boost the electronic music scene. Wan, the owner of

Baba, one of the nicest guys you will ever meet, has a passion for electronic music which has brought a new wave of fans from Thailand, which I believe will get bigger for many years to come. It was a perfect start to my Thai adventure. Everything was going so well, but then I made a mistake, which will stay with me for the rest of my life.

After Circoloco, many of my friends left Phuket; many went back to Europe. Dubfire was arriving a week later, so I would be alone. I had met a girl in Lithuania a few months before I left for Asia, and we had been talking for a while. She had never left Europe before, let alone visited Thailand, and she wanted to come and join me. I hesitated at first. She was always cool when we met up but inviting someone so far away was a bit risky. One night after a few Singhas, I was talking to her and booked her a flight. She flew the next day from Lithuania and landed the following morning, where I met her at the airport.

The airline, Aeroflot, lost her luggage, so she arrived with almost nothing. I took her to a store to get some essentials until her case arrived the next day. The alarm bells rang when she did a sweep of the store, filling her basket with the most expensive cosmetics she could find — hundreds of euros worth of creams, then she stood there waiting for my credit card. The warning signs were already there.

We arrived at the hotel. She needed something to wear that day and evening. Yet another sweep of the hotel boutique, grabbing six bikinis and a sarong. "Why do you need all of that? You'll have your things in the morning," I said. I was already annoyed. She put most of it back but kept the most expensive bikini and charged it to my room — more warning signs.

We checked into the villa. It was something special. Total five-star luxury, ultra-modern. Villas have their own private pool. It was one of the most beautiful locations I have ever stayed with the famous Thai hospitality.

The first few days with the girl were fine. Her luggage arrived the next morning, she was relaxed, and we were both happy to be in such a paradise. She told me that it was the first time she had seen such happy, genuine people in her life, only able to compare it to the dark mood of the people where she came from. It was all massages, sunsets, beautiful food, beach life and cocktails. It couldn't have been going any better. After a few days, though, everything changed.

We woke up one day and went down to the hotel pool. Out of nothing, she turned very moody, anger somehow appearing from nowhere. I asked what was wrong. After a few times asking, she finally told me. She was suffering from depression. This particular mood had come on because the waiter hadn't brought her the cocktail that she wanted. I had a few friends around the pool who came to say hello; she completely ignored them. I told her that this was not cool.

I am someone who gives good energy to everyone, and I expect that to be returned to me. I can't have someone around being moody and having to make excuses for them. I told her to stop and be nice to people. She said that she was going back to the villa alone for a while, and she left. I did some work on my laptop around the pool before returning home.

I walked in to find her sitting on the floor, cross-legged, making a video on her phone. Her eyes were distant; she looked drugged. I asked what she was doing. She told me that I had walked in on her as she had been making a suicide video, and she had just overdosed on her depression pills. I grabbed her phone and checked the video. She wasn't lying; it was indeed a suicide video. I checked her washbag, which had been in her lost luggage. It contained several strips of pills, but as they were written in Lithuanian and Russian, I had no idea what they were. Many were empty. I asked her if she really had overdosed or if she was just lying for attention. She seemed to be so drugged that she couldn't answer me.

We were very remote. The nearest hospital was hours away, and in Thailand, you don't want to cause an unnecessary scene. Thais sweep any drama under the carpet so as not to affect tourism. Just a few days before, in the condo where I was living, a Chinese child had fallen from the balcony to his death, and nobody knew about it; nothing was in the news. They were told to keep quiet. One of my neighbours had seen the ambulance and told me a few days later. I knew that I had to play the situation carefully.

She seemed to be holding up; perhaps I had walked in at the right time before she had taken too many pills. I told her to lie down, and I sat at the dining table working on my laptop, keeping an eye on her. I was checking on her every thirty minutes. She was sleeping and breathing fine, so I continued working.

I looked up again after a few hours. She had suddenly vanished from the bed. I ran into the bedroom, and she wasn't there. I was running around the villa and couldn't find her anywhere. I walked out of the patio doors to the private pool, and there she was — submerged under the water, her skin almost blue and her eyes white. I jumped into the pool and pulled her out. I felt her pulse. Her heart was still beating; she was still breathing. Again, I was trying to work out if she had actually tried to drown herself or if it was just for attention, as it is in most suicide cases. She was coherent, and she told me that she was OK, but she was shaking with cold, so I told her to go to the bathroom for a hot shower and come back. I kept a close eye on the door. This time I stayed right next to her on the bed. If she tried to run away, I would know, but she fell fast asleep all night and woke up next morning.

She woke up and asked me what had happened the day before; she didn't seem to remember. I told her and said that it wasn't going to work out. I should book her a new flight back to Lithuania, departing later that day. She agreed, and I booked the flight.

We started packing up our things, as we had to check out of the hotel at midday. I came out of the bathroom, and I heard the door slam shut. She had run out of the front door. I went out to look for her but couldn't find anyone; the hotel staff hadn't seen her either. I went back in and continued to pack up my stuff and hers, as it was check-out time. I packed everything up and just sat there waiting. Her phone was in the villa, so I couldn't call her, but I knew she would come back. Maybe she had gone to buy a gift to take back for her mother, as she said that she needed to. I waited until after midday. It got to the point if we hadn't left soon, she would have missed the flight. Little did I know that this was her whole ploy.

She was down at the beach, hiding and waiting until it was so late that she would miss the flight. She eventually came back, looking like a drowned rat. She said that she had been swimming in the sea and had tried to drown herself, but it had been too difficult, so she had come back. By now, I had lost all respect for her, and I just wanted to get her on a flight home. I told her that we had to leave as the check-out time had passed and she had probably missed her flight, but we could still make it if we went now. She told me that she needed a shower before leaving, so she went into the bathroom, and I waited in the living room, watching the door.

I could hear the hairdryer whirring in the bathroom, but the sound was getting lower and lower. It sounded suspicious, so I went into the bathroom and found her with the hairdryer under the tap, trying to electrocute herself. I ran in and pulled the hairdryer out of her hand. She ran to the kitchen and grabbed the sharpest knife that she could find, jumped into the pool, and tried to stab herself in the stomach. The scene was just unbelievable. I realised that I had a seriously mentally unstable person on my hands.

She was just trying to kill herself in any way possible, and I was trying to stop her. Again, I jumped into the pool, pulled the knife out of her hand, and pulled her out of the water. I locked all of the knives in the safe. I told her that I was going to call the hotel security and we would be going to the hospital immediately. I found the manager, who told me that before we contacted any police or ambulance, he would go and calm her down. I sat outside for about thirty minutes while he spoke to her. Whatever he said to her, it appeared to work. She suddenly came around, became very calm and agreed to leave the hotel.

We checked out of the hotel and went to Phuket Airport. We arrived and went to the Aeroflot office. She had just missed her flight, but they said she could take the next one in a few hours. The Aeroflot lady was Chinese, but she spoke Russian, so the girl started talking to her in Russian in front of me purposely so that I couldn't understand. I did understand the gist of it however. It was on the lines of 'this is my boyfriend, we just had an argument, please don't change my flight, he will be ok in a few hours. With that, I said goodbye and took a taxi to my condo. She could wait for the next flight without me. I'd had enough of the whole drama; I couldn't do any more.

I texted her to see if she had got through security OK, but her phone was off. I arrived at my condo and was working on my laptop around the pool but wondering if she was OK. I tried calling her, but her phone was still off. I assumed that she was already on the flight.

Six hours later, I received a message from a friend in Phuket. It was a link to *the Phuket News*. The headline of the article was: "Lithuanian Woman saved from jump at Phuket Airport". My heart stopped. I just sat there staring at the screen. There was a video that an onlooker had taken of the girl who I thought was on her flight back home, but she never took the flight. She had walked back out of the airport after I left and was standing on the edge of Phuket Airport bridge — a bridge of fifty metres high, which six people have jumped from to their death in the past. I guess some people don't like leaving Phuket.

She had been standing on the wall of the bridge; a local taxi driver was trying to persuade her to come down. It went on for over thirty minutes. She was facing him, listening, then suddenly turned around and put her arms out to jump. He quickly grabbed her legs and pulled her down, hundreds of onlookers screaming. That's when the video stopped. I just sat there staring at the screen, wondering what had happened and where she was now.

One hour later, I received a text. It was her. She was in a psychiatric hospital, sectioned and on suicide watch. She was begging me to come and release her. I had no idea what to do. These were uncharted waters for me.

I sat there thinking for hours. I told her that it couldn't be me who released her. She had tried to kill herself several times with me, so it had to be someone else, but she didn't know anyone in Thailand. She texted me every hour all evening, begging me to come, but visiting hours were already over for the day, and they wouldn't have let me in if I tried. During the night, she sent me a video of a patient in the ward trying to attack her; security doing nothing to stop it. A third patient — a pregnant woman — stepped in and saved her. It was all too much. I got on my motorbike and went to the hospital.

It took a while for me to find the suicide ward. Nobody spoke English. I eventually found it, and I saw her through a window. I was not allowed inside. I had to talk to her from outside, through iron bars, like visiting a prisoner. I could see the small ward with three other women. One I recognised as the woman who tried to kill her the night before, the pregnant one who saved her, and another woman who was sleeping. The security guard was at the top, not once looking to see what was going on.

I took her some water, mango, and other fruits from the local market. I took the sticks out of the fruits just in case, possibly a little extreme, but I had to make sure. I was standing in the blazing thirty-three degrees Celsius talking to her through the bars. She was begging me to get her out, it was really difficult, but I had to tell her that I couldn't be the one to get her out. It had to be someone else, either a family member or a security guard, who could fly with her back to Lithuania. Her mother had spoken to her and was trying to take time off work to fly out to Phuket to pick her up. She didn't speak English, so I couldn't call her, but they were speaking to each other continually, trying to find a solution.

I asked if she had travel insurance — stupid question. Travel insurance doesn't include suicide. Whichever way we got out of this, it was a mess. Why didn't she just get on the flight? How did it escalate to this level over a cocktail? Was going back home to Lithuania so bad? So many questions that I couldn't answer.

After ninety minutes, the staff told me my time was up. My face was red from standing in the blazing sun. I rode back to my condo on my bike, trying to process what was going on. I asked some friends what I should do. "Just leave her there," they said. "You've done everything you can." They were right; she was clearly psychotic, she didn't want to help herself, but I couldn't leave her there. I had to help her to get home somehow.

Back in Lithuania, it was mid-winter, dark and minus fifteen degrees Celsius. She was now implying that she wanted to stay and continue the trip in Thailand, as the thought of going back there was depressing her as much as being in the hospital. Somehow, with a quick mood swing, she had managed to change the most perfect luxury holiday into this: standing behind bars in a mental asylum being attacked by patients.

I received a message from her that night saying that her mother was going to fly out twenty-four hours later to pick her up. What a relief. I offered to pay for a hotel for them to stay in. Her mother had planned to fly out, pick her up from the hospital, and then fly directly back to Lithuania on the same day. It would have been too much; I offered her the choice of hotels, and she chose one (the most expensive one, of course). The next day, her mother arrived and collected her from the hospital. By now, it was big news in Phuket, and my phone didn't stop buzzing.

A few hours later, she and her mother were sending me photos from the hotel pool. They looked like a mother and daughter on a normal family holiday, except that she had become quite famous for her attempted jump off the bridge. Everywhere she went, the local Thai people, even the police, wanted photos with her. It was all very bizarre.

The taxi driver who had saved her from the suicide jump was given an award from the local mayor, which was also on the news. The police offered to give her and her mother an escort from the hotel to the airport. I guess to make sure that she flew out this time.

She asked if I would ride to the hotel to say goodbye before the police came. I wasn't sure if it was a good idea, but I went. She was fragile, and I didn't want any more problems. I saw her just for a few minutes before the police showed up. It was so strange to see someone who, just a few days before, I had seen behind bars and, just a day before that, had tried to commit suicide. Perhaps I shouldn't have gone, but it felt like the right thing to do.

Sure enough, the police escort arrived. They took them right through airport security, dozens of people taking photos. They were upgraded to business class by Aeroflot, where attempted suicide seemingly gets you a guaranteed upgrade. The whole thing was a complete debacle.

Next day, she texted me to say that she'd arrived back home in freezing Lithuania. She checked herself into rehab. I continued my time in Thailand, trying to forget all of the drama that had just happened.

Dubfire and another friend of mine, Kevin, arrived in Phuket just at the right time. I needed some good people around. I told them the whole story. Dubfire has some mad tour stories, but Kevin is a riot. He has some tales that make my jaw drop, but on this occasion, mine was unbeatable. It was so good to have some old friends in town. I was starting to lose faith in humans. Dubfire played a great event on the beach; we hung out for some days doing guy things — spa, gym, boats and good food with not a girl in sight. It was perfect.

After that incident, I closed up. I wouldn't talk to anyone other than close friends for a long time. I started to doubt my instinct, which has always served me well over the years from being so well travelled. I've met so many people from around the world that I can usually spot a bad person from the start, but this time I had totally fucked up.

I tried to look on the funny side. I could now say that I jumped into a pool to save a drowning woman, the hero taxi driver had a certificate on his mantlepiece, the girl's mother had a surprise two-day trip to Thailand, everyone was still in one piece. *But* it could have been so different.

I stayed in Thailand for an extended period and laid low. Of all the things that have happened to me over the years on the road, this was the one that affected me the most. I got my head down and worked on my projects for the months ahead — definitely staying away from women. Most of the women in Thailand, either ladyboys or prostitutes. It's better not to talk to any at all. Despite what happened, I still love Thailand and Asia and will keep coming back.

The rest of my trip to Thailand was smooth. More DJs came out for some cool events in Phuket and Koh

Phangan. I went on to Kuala Lumpur, Singapore, and Bali to visit some venues and meet with promoters to plan some gigs. I came back to Europe when winter was over. I told myself that I needed to calm down for a while.

When it all Catches up with You

It was the end of my Asia trip, and I was feeling better than ever. Three months in Asia, eventful, but I was healthy and had experienced good food, sports and lots of sun. I was recharged for the summer of 2019.

I had two of my artists playing on the same weekend: one in Bangkok and the other in Kiev. Somehow, I made it to both events. I still had the fire inside me. I had missed touring. It was so good to be in a European club again, and spring was a perfect time to come back. I stayed a few days in Kiev; it was almost surreal to be back in Europe again. Tall people, blonde girls, I hadn't seen this since the year before. A quick stop in Wales, and it was on to one of my favourite festivals in the world: Sunwaves in Romania.

Sunwaves is an amazing festival. Based in Mamaia on the Romanian coast, it's the first major outdoor festival of the European clubbing calendar. It's based on the beach; party people come from all over the world. Like always, I booked my last trip at the last minute, and most of the hotels were full. The best one I could find was old and shabby, but Sunwaves is five days non-stop. I would hardly ever be at the hotel, so I was fine with it. It was so nice to be at a festival again. I saw so many people I hadn't seen for a long time.

After five days of partying, I flew back to London. The flight was full of zombies from the festival — most of them still wired. Many were coughing and sneezing. I remember thinking, *I hope I don't catch anything.*

Sure enough, the next day, I woke up and felt like shit. I had flu-like symptoms, but on a much bigger scale than I had ever felt before. Like always, I didn't go to the doctor; I tried to beat it naturally and continued to work. The weeks went by, and I was deteriorating fast. After one month, I was confined to my bed. No amount of ginger and lemon would cure this. Something wasn't right.

Finally, I called a doctor who diagnosed me with severe pneumonia. My lungs were full of fluid, and my body was shutting down. He couldn't believe I had gone so long without treatment. A common cause of pneumonia is dirty air-conditioners. The hotel in Romania had an old one that had been rattling away the whole time. I shouldn't have even turned it on, but the room was so hot.

I had never been sick before in my life. It was ironic that after all the hard years of touring, my immune system had stood up to everything, but as soon as I had a break and took it a bit easier, I couldn't fight off a simple infection from a hotel air conditioner.

The doctor gave me strong antibiotics, but after one week, I was getting worse again and was rushed to hospital. I didn't even know where the nearest hospital was; I had never been to one. They had no record of me other than when I was born in 1976. The doctors there gave me another X-ray which showed that my lungs were still full of infection. They doubled my dose of antibiotics. Two days later, I was back in hospital, all wired up. The nurse gave me the news. I'd had a heart attack.

My heart couldn't handle the strength of the antibiotics. I was having strong palpitations with the pneumonia, so when I did have the attack, I didn't even know. It was as if my body was finally giving up after the hard fifteen years that I had punished it from touring. I cancelled all work; I was down on the ground. I had a few stints in and out of hospital. It took me three months to totally recover.

I remember lying at home, watching TV. Sasha sent me a message asking how I was. He had heard about my illness and sent me his best wishes. "All those years of hard touring catch up on us eventually," he said. "Take more care of yourself." I will always remember these words from the man who inspired me to get into music in the first place. It was the pick-up that I needed after sitting alone for so long.

Eventually, I recovered, but a new problem had arisen. The doctors had also prescribed sedatives to get me through the pain and help me sleep. I had been taking pills for several years for flights, jetlag, and to regulate sleeping while flying through time zones. It's normal on tour, but now I was taking up to nine per day: 90 mg to get me through the pain. If I tried to stop taking them, I would get huge withdrawal symptoms — all kinds of symptoms: panic attacks, tremors, anxiety, hallucinations.

The only way to stop the withdrawals was by taking more pills. It was a cycle that I couldn't get out of. This went on for several more months, long after I had recovered from the illness. I had several chances to go back on tour, but I couldn't. I couldn't leave my house for more than three hours before the withdrawal symptoms started again. I managed to DJ at two gigs. For both, I was completely sedated through my whole set, even hallucinating at times, but in the dark club, nobody noticed anything.

I drove right across Europe from east to west. A two-day drive, taking eight pills when the withdrawals came on. I had a serious problem that I had to fix, and there was only one way to get me out of it: rehab.

Rehab

As you can imagine, in my industry, I know quite a few people who have ended up in rehab for various things, from alcoholism to drugs to sex addiction. I never imagined that I would be one of them. I researched what I needed to do, called up a few places and checked in the next day. It wasn't a nice way to spend Christmas.

I needed a detox centre, it's the first stage of rehab for many, but it's all I needed. I found one in Wales. It felt right to do this in my own country. I didn't tell anyone. I wanted to fix it before anyone knew. To tell someone you are sick is a weakness. To tell someone that you conquered is a strength.

The day I was due to check in, I received a very sad call. My old friend Paul, "The Mad Mohawk", who gave me my first ever break in music, both as a DJ and in PR, had committed suicide in Sydney. I had never felt so down in my life. I couldn't get my head around it. Paul was one of the kindest people I've ever known. Hardworking, honest and decent. Such an inspiration to me that I've dedicated this book to him. I had to process this news on a four-hour train ride to rehab. I took more pills.

The train ride was horrendous. Packed with people going home for Christmas. Hot and uncomfortable. One guy near me had a heart attack in his seat. The train was stopped, he was given CPR right next to me in the aisle. I had a panic attack, couldn't leave my seat. I had to take two more pills.

The train arrived. I couldn't wait to get off. I was struggling. A nurse came to pick me up, and we drove through the country roads, away from civilisation. We entered the grounds of a huge mansion. It looked very grand. Not what I expected.

I walked in, and the doctor checked me over. He asked me to hold my hands in front of me, which were shaking like leaves. "Give that man an injection," he said to the nurse. "He's having a fit." The nurse gave me an injection, and I immediately calmed down. I was taken to my room. A tiny box with a plastic bed and sink. No Wi-Fi or phone signal. It would be my home for the next two weeks. Not too dissimilar to the jail cell I was in just a few years before.

I imagined that I would be in there with other people with similar conditions, but I was the only one hooked on prescribed meds. Everyone was an alcoholic or a heroin addict. I had nothing in common with anyone, apart from the withdrawal symptoms which were the same as theirs. One of the first things I was asked was, "What are you in here for?" It felt like jail. The worrying thing was that everyone else had been in before, except for me. This was a scary thought.

The first forty-eight hours were absolute hell. I was awake for the whole time; the withdrawal symptoms were immense. This was the worst pain I had ever experienced. The doctors gave me alternative meds every four hours to numb the pain but warned me that the first three days would be difficult. They were not joking. The first night, I was on suicide watch. Every hour, my door would open, a nurse would check I was alive, then the door would shut. The similarities to jail were remarkably similar.

The other patients were constantly on edge. Relaxed when their medication was taking effect, then they would become edgy when it started to fade. Two guys were talking totally calmly to each other at the dinner table, then suddenly flipped and started to fight — plates and dishes smashed on the floor, and food went everywhere. I never found out why.

After that, I stayed in my room as much as possible, only going to the communal area for meals. Everyone had to sit and eat together. I used to eat my food as fast as possible, wash my dishes and get back in my room. When the other patients asked me what I did for a living, I told them about my life on tour. They were fascinated, sitting up straight, as I told them my stories. One of them commented that it was no surprise that I had ended up there.

I tried to be polite and ask them about their lives, but they had nothing to tell other than how much heroin they had done or how much booze they had drunk in one session. I felt like a total alien, counting the days until I got out.

After the fifth day, my condition improved. I asked the doctor if I could leave after two more days. I couldn't imagine spending Christmas in there. He said he would decide on the final day. That was a long wait, sitting in my room alone, wondering if I would be stuck there for Christmas or allowed out into the world. I sat looking out of my window for hours. I saw nothing but thick grey fog and rain. It was as depressing as it gets. What had my life come to?

Day seven came, and the doctor came to give me the assessment. He gave me the all-clear to leave. It was 23 December. I said goodbye to the patients. I felt sorry for them having to spend Christmas in there. Some were at the start of a three-month stint.

I remember walking out. I felt a sense of freedom that I hadn't experienced since that day I had the call from my lawyer to tell me that the police had dropped the charges. I was driven out of the grounds and never looked back. I never wanted to see that place again. I wanted to be the first one who didn't return.

I took the train from North to South Wales, a four-hour journey, stopping at every village. It was strange to see people who were behaving normally — professionals on their way back home for Christmas. I felt paranoid that they knew where I had come from, nervous whenever anyone looked at me.

I stared out of the window almost the whole way back. I had never travelled the length of my own country before. Beautiful rolling hills and dense forest. The sun stayed low, flickering through the trees, flashing the carriage like strobe lights in a club. It was mid-winter's day, never really light, usually quite depressing, but for me, it felt like a new life was starting.

It hit me that I was now a very different person from the one who started the year. I started to be grateful for many things that I took for granted before. Rehab had given me time to think about myself and what to do with my life. I had so many ideas which had never come to me before. Finally, I would get my book finished. I would make some new music and start a new concept. It was Christmas time and a good time to reflect.

The train pulled into my hometown. Newport is an ugly city. I've always hated it, but the feeling of familiarity was comforting. I checked into the Celtic Manor Resort. It's a famous hotel in my hometown where I had always wanted to stay. I laid down on the huge bed. It was so comfortable compared to the cheap plastic single one I had slept in for the past week. I was used to staying at the top hotels in the world but never really appreciated them. Now I was savouring every moment. I went down to the spa and pool. It was so nice being able to walk around, exercise, eat the food I like. When it gets taken away from you, you appreciate it much more.

I had lost my reality, stuck in the bubble of the DJ life. Now I take nothing for granted. I've become a much better person than I was before. I no longer get the red mist; I don't care about many of the materialistic things that seemed to be so important before: expensive clothes, watches, et cetera. I got rid of my car, I got back to the simple life, and I felt much happier. The year 2019 had been the worst year of my life. The first year I hadn't been to Ibiza since 1994, I'd hardly travelled anywhere. It was the first time I had ever been seriously ill, and my first time in rehab. I couldn't wait for the new year to start. I was totally ready for 2020.

2020

I'm not even giving this chapter a proper title. There are no words for it. What can I say? 2020. It had such a nice ring to it. A new decade. New beginnings. It was going to be my year. It started so well. I spent January back in my beloved Thailand; I didn't invite anyone this time. I was totally revitalised. I made some new music which was sounding good. I was excited for the first time in a while.

There were rumours of a virus coming in from Wuhan; my friends and I passed it off. There were many tourists from Wuhan staying in our condos. We would make jokes: holding our breath in the elevator when they got in and only breathing out after they walked out, going to breakfast before they would arrive. Local bars would do ironic promotions with Corona beer. It was all for fun. Borders with China were soon closed, and those who were in Thailand were sent back. It would just be like other viruses, contained at the source and disappear, surely.

February came, Thailand was getting quiet. Tourists were cancelling their trips out of fear. I moved on to Singapore. This was when I realised that the situation was serious. I wore a mask for the first time. I didn't even know how to put it on. Places were closing down, events were being cancelled. I started to worry. My livelihood was music. If this virus got worse, our global scene would be affected. It already was happening in Asia right in front of my eyes. I went for dinner with a promoter in Singapore who wanted to cancel our event. I persuaded him to go ahead, but hardly anyone showed up. People were scared. I went on to Bali, which was more relaxed, but we could sense something was coming.

I flew back to London on 29 February. Artbat were in town, two of my favourite artists. I went with them to Printworks — monster of a night — wall-to-wall packed. Everything seemed normal, but it turned out to be a super-spreader event. Within a week, the whole world stopped, pretty much overnight.

The same virus I had been running from in Asia for the last two months had seemingly followed me back to Europe. Unprecedented in peacetime, every music venue closed down. I watched the whole music industry decimated right in front of my eyes. I had worked in music since 1995. What would I do now?

I felt depressed for a few days. I felt like the whole world was falling in around me. My friends and family were catching the virus. It was still unknown. I was considered high-risk due to my recent health problems, so I isolated myself for several months from the whole world. It was the second lockdown in two years for me after my own personal one in 2019. I couldn't believe it was happening again. This time everyone else was in it with me.

One day, I woke up and had a new outlook. I would make something positive out of this. I cancelled my Netflix account. No TV, gaming or YouTube. I didn't want distractions; I wasn't going to waste this time. Instead, I would use it to build a new future. It was clear that gigs and festivals were not going to open until at least 2021. I needed to learn something new.

My three favourite things: music, restaurants, and travel, were all taken away from me. My wanderlust and free spirit confiscated. I was confined to my apartment. The first thing I did was to buy some home exercise equipment. An active body goes with an active mind. The gym was closed, but I would make my own.

The last time my work was affected by something like this was the Iceland volcano in 2010. I remember having all gigs cancelled for several weeks. Before that, it was the global financial crisis, during which we took a big hit. Entertainment is not recession proof, as we all know. I had to learn things. I took a course in e-commerce, videography, digital marketing. I could do this until music came back, and they could work in tandem.

Studying again was tough. Twenty-five years after I first went to university, my brain had been on autopilot. I had to wake it up. I sat for weeks and weeks, going over it again and again. I spoke to many of my DJ friends. Many were depressed. I felt sorry for everyone in music.

For many, the best part of being a DJ is the fame and adoration. Being the centre of attention can be addictive. The control you feel when you have thousands of people in front of you dancing to your sound is unparalleled. When this is taken away from you, you can lose all self-esteem. When those gigs and tours are taken away, you question your worth.

The lockdown went on for so long. In London, it was the longest in Europe. Four months. I got to a point where I couldn't even imagine going out to a party. I was getting used to doing everything at home, but I was missing travelling, the new cultures, my friends around the world. I would video call at least one of them every day, which kept me going.

Covid changed the entertainment industry forever. It will never be the same again. We are always the last of industries to come back in recessions and pandemics. From March 2020, every festival was cancelled until 2021. It will go down as the worst year ever for musicians and entertainers. But we have all learnt some valuable lessons: Don't throw all your eggs into one basket. Nothing is forever. Always evolve and never sit on your laurels.

I had to take a good look at how I was living my life. It was so fast paced; I never had the chance to stop and reflect. You never move on as a person if you don't continuously assess yourself. It took being hospitalised,

239

rehab, and two lockdowns to stop me in my tracks. I had been living a wild life. I don't regret anything, but it was time to calm down. Covid also brought out the worst in many people. Some countries like Mexico, Greece, Egypt were continuing to do events throughout the pandemic. Many of the DJ's needed the work so would go and play there. Then we noticed the sudden 'call-out' culture where online trolls would say 'So and so DJ is playing in Tulum, how can he be so irresponsible?' What they don't realise is that DJs need to make money, after one year many of their savings had run out, so if they had the chance to play in a country where it was allowed to have events, then why not? But of course, the lucky people who didn't lose their jobs, sitting at home furloughed and getting paid, were as bitter and twisted as usual and trying to bring these guys down who were just trying to make a living. This appalled me how jealous and warped people can be. Some positives came out of the pandemic however. Some of the best music that was ever made was produced when artists were stuck at home unable to travel. People had chance to stop and re-structure their businesses properly rather than running them with no plan or direction as had been happening for years.

"Why Does Everything Happen to You?"

So why *does* everything happen to me?

It took writing this book to fully realise. My inner sense of adventure takes me outside the comfort zone. I love to take risks and put myself out there among new people and places. I've met the most amazing souls by taking chances on strangers and trusting my instinct, but also, I have discovered many pitfalls. I'm not the kind of character who likes to stay at home or in the safety of the hotel room until the promoter comes to pick me up. That's boring. Especially when travelling, I like to get among it and challenge myself. Sometimes it works out; sometimes it goes horribly wrong.

Once I had time to sit down and write, it was a big reflection for me on the last fifteen crazy years. For sure, there will be more wild times to come. I'm not getting any younger, but I still have my sense of adventure, and I love to go out and listen to music. My father went out dancing on Saturday nights until he was eighty-three, albeit a different kind of dancing. I'm from a family who lives for the weekend and counts down the days until the next one. I still make music and love to play it out, and this, combined with my love of travel, means that the adventures will keep coming.

I have no idea what is around the corner for me; this obscure lifestyle can take you anywhere. If someone had told me back in 1995 when I got into electronic music that three decades later, we would still be dancing to the same 4/4 beat, I would never have believed them. It's lasted much longer than anyone imagined.

If you look at disco, punk, rock and roll, et cetera, all had their shelf life, but I believe that 4/4 is the most natural beat to dance to and hence it will always be here. Constant technological advances ensure music continues to improve. Easier access to software enables more and more quality music to be made. Before, you needed a big studio full of expensive equipment to make music. Now, you need just a laptop, software and some headphones.

Social media has played a big part in music's popularity; videos of DJs playing go viral in minutes, streams like Cercle have brought the clubbing experience into people's houses. Those who can't make it to events can still watch from home. It's a far cry from the days when I used to go hunting through record shops for live DJ mixes on cassette because I couldn't get into clubs. It used to be the only way that I could hear the music. Now, the music is mainstream and accessible to everyone, and it won't go away.

The music scene now is better organised with more professional people running the best clubs and agencies.

Sure, there are still a lot of chancers out there and a lot of wild characters, but I couldn't imagine not working in the industry that I have been involved with since 1995. When you make your passion your livelihood and combine it with travelling, it can't get any better.

There are only a handful of countries in the world now which I have never been to, and I'm determined to complete the whole set, just in a less hectic way. I've almost run out of new cultures to explore, but I want to see those that I have missed so far. People often say to me that I am lucky to work with what I love, but anyone can do it if they make that jump.

You have one life. Live it.